Kind words *

Beautifully written Paul. I really
so many of these adventures,
simpler, happier time. You truly
I urge you to have these publishe.. ... .
for an editor, so don't let anyone take liberties with this manuscript.

Steve - *Santa Rosa, California*

What a treat you have given me in sending me a copy of your book!! Why
has it taken you so long to blossom out in the delightful writer that you truly
are? You have a gift of words that had me laughing particularly in "Olympics
in the front yard". I started reading it when I was at the beauty parlor and
Sandy, the hairdresser, said she must read that book that had me in stitches.
I am almost at the end, and plan to re-read it afterwards. I hope you
continue to write. You have been blessed with a great gift.

Valda - *Fort Lauderdale, Florida*

I sit here after reading the "Summer of 1956" with eyes full of tears for those
long ago days when life seemed so uncomplicated, and the people one knew
were the "genuine article", it makes me very grateful to have been able to
share these moments. Thank you so much for sharing these wonderful
memories.

Herb - *Oakville, Canada*

I am floored not just by the stories but by the beauty and sensitivity of your
writing. You have mastered the ability to write in the first person, a very
difficult thing to do. The humor in the "Bulrush" and "Christopher's Car" is so
well depicted and then you switch to a more sensitive tone in the beautiful
piece on "The Swan" and the requiem to your friend in "Hanging with Ian".

Sara - *Atlanta, Georgia*

This is just a note to let you know that I really did enjoy reading your
collection of short stories of life in Jamaica from the mid 1950s to the mid
1960s. You express yourself very well and I love the way you have drawn
meaning from the varied experiences you have had growing up in Jamaica.
As I read it I couldn't help thinking about my own growing-up in Jamaica at
that time. It is definitely worth publishing and I hope you will do so.

John - *Charleston, South Carolina*

Thank you so much for sending those wonderful experiences of your "youth"
in Jamaica. I have greatly enjoyed them. It brought back so many memories
of my own life, and I remember so many people & places. We spent many a
day at Llandovery, and Dad used to spend days at a time with Sam and
others there - fishing by night, and sleeping in a thatched hut during the day!

I think that was his idea of Heaven - cooking fish and roasting breadfruit and green plantain over an open fire. Liz - *Toronto, Canada*

I have just finished reading your book and it is a masterpiece of writing. It should find a ready market from a Caribbean market at home and abroad, that will "eat it up!" Before Day a' Mawnin' is a magnificent depiction of life and activity in Jamaica in the middle of the 20th century. The detailed descriptions of a host of locations, farm life routines and equipment, country schooling, native trees and fruits, and much more, brings back wonderful memories to the older generations, while opening up the past to the younger.
Peter - *Toronto, Canada*

The stories are so evocative and the account of the Coombs barbeque and those T bone steaks have lingered on the periphery of my memory for years. I have to say that it has imprinted in my memory all these years as no steak has ever tasted as good since. I don't remember the chef, but I can remember the chill of the water, the cloudiness, and the shadows the leaves made on the pools of water and the fact that the water was so shallow that even mom forgot to fuss that we might drown if she took her eyes of us.
Rosy - *Edinburgh, Scotland*

The other cause for delay was to find the right words to respond to "Before Day a Mawnin". Really enjoyed it! As boys at the same time, there were so many parallel and apparently intersecting experiences. I had seen the chapter title "Hanging with Ian" and hadn't given it any more thought until properly arriving at it in chronological sequence. I was completely blown away - I knew Ian well - and spent quite a lot of time in his company in those early days when he was first at BNS and constantly wrecking cars.
Richard - Kingston, Jamaica

I returned home yesterday after being with the family during the holidays and have read and re-read your "Tribute to Ian". It is just wonderful, a real keeper, and as my Dad would say "you could go into the pulpit and preach a good sermon!" What a set of fun loving mischievous young people you all were. I don't know how Uncle Bas & Aunt Monica survived you kids! Laughed all the way through your composition, and think it would make an excellent movie. Liz - *Toronto, Canada*

I just finished the story you sent about the Broken Bulrush. Great story man. I think folks like Josiah are the real rural Jamaicans of yesteryear. City folk in our days in Jamaica could not touch the real character we met in the little backwater places like Jericho and Mosquito Cove or Kitson Town. I would not trade my experiences in rural Jamaica with anything that I have seen since.
Chris- Boca Raton, Florida

It is as if we had existed in a parallel universe, I genuinely had no idea until now what a more exciting life you actually had than either Mary or myself. I can remember the tales of Mr. Gore keeping a crocodile in his yard, but thought that it was a rural myth, either way the man was deranged.

Ros*y - Edinburgh, Scotland*

I thoroughly enjoyed the book ! Your description of hiking to Blue Mtn. was so good that I could actually feel like I was there!

Nancy - Tampa, Florida

I can't begin to tell you how much I enjoyed reading your book! It brought back so many childhood memories of living in Jamaica. Also, there were people mentioned throughout with whom I am acquainted. I am sure that if you had your book published it would be a best seller, especially with Jamaicans born in the 1940,s. Even Fred enjoyed listening to many parts which I read to him. Your descriptions of events and scenery are entertaining and full of imagery. Thanks again, and Congrats!!!

Shirley – Kingston, Ontario

"Before Day a Mawnin" what a lovely surprise! Many thanks for these short stories about life in rural Jamaica. I have been reading the stories "slowly". Will share with Daddy when I am through.

Faith - Kingston, Jamaica

Before Day a' Mawnin'
Growing up in the enchanted island of Jamaica

For information, address Paul Virtue, 3420 Kennebuck Court, Raleigh, NC 27613, USA. Email pvirtue@prodigy.net.

Original Publication - 2009

Direct Purchases: www.paulvirtuebooks.com
email: paul@paulvirtuebooks.com

ISBN 978-0-578-04234-3

51800

9 780578 042343

$18.00

I dedicate this book to my wife, Olivene Veronica, who is my best friend, lover and the fellow traveler through life.

Before Day a' Mawnin'

Growing up in the enchanted island of Jamaica

by
Paul Douglas Virtue

Family Tree

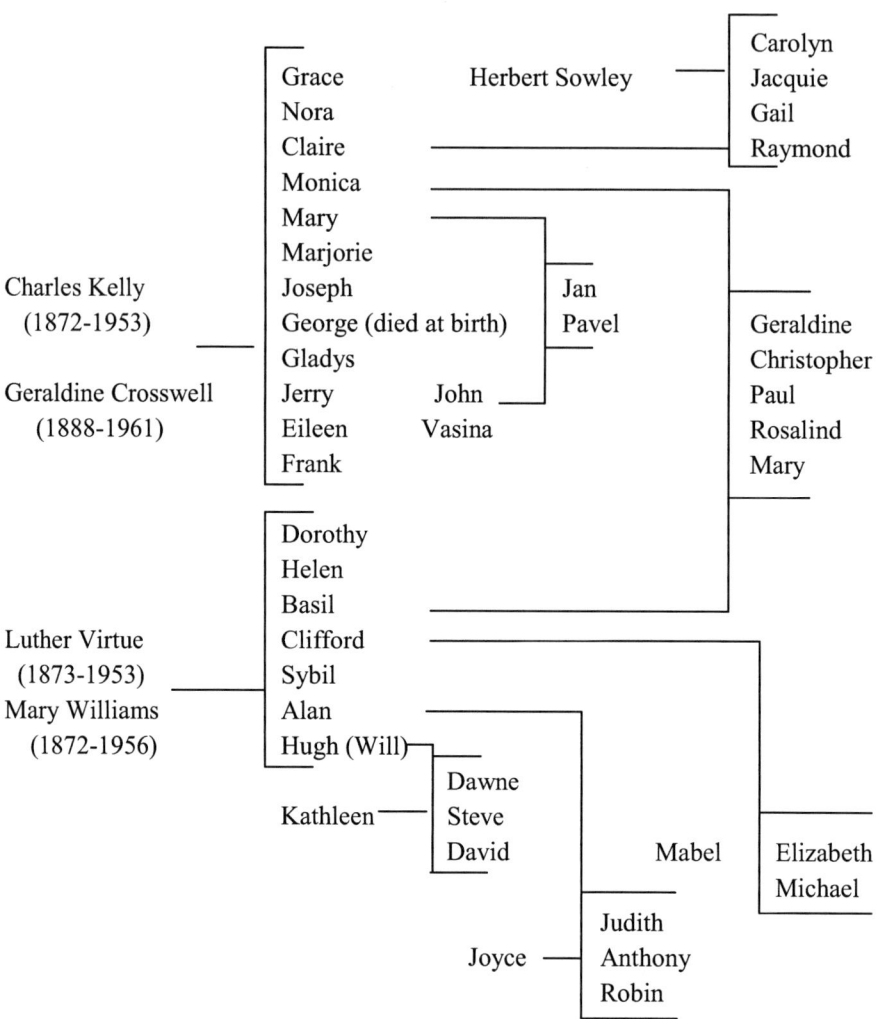

Charles Kelly
(1872-1953)

Geraldine Crosswell
(1888-1961)

Grace
Nora
Claire
Monica
Mary
Marjorie
Joseph
George (died at birth)
Gladys
Jerry
Eileen
Frank

Herbert Sowley

Carolyn
Jacquie
Gail
Raymond

Jan
Pavel

John
Vasina

Geraldine
Christopher
Paul
Rosalind
Mary

Luther Virtue
(1873-1953)
Mary Williams
(1872-1956)

Dorothy
Helen
Basil
Clifford
Sybil
Alan
Hugh (Will)

Kathleen

Dawne
Steve
David

Joyce

Mabel

Judith
Anthony
Robin

Elizabeth
Michael

Inside

Illustrations and Maps

Photographs

Maps

Foreword

*B*efore day 'a Mawning is Jamaican for the dawn of a new day. It is when fishermen and farmers do most of their heavy work; but more so it is a metaphor for the coming of age of a youngster and for Jamaica as it faced the sunrise of political independence and the ending of a colonial past.

This book has been fifteen years in the making, starting as a series of short stories written to preserve memories of mid-20th century life in rural Jamaica. What started out as an indulgence to my children has grown over the years, and at the urging of friends with whom I had shared some of the stories, these are now complied into a simple book. The stories will resonate with West Indians from this same era, yet they should also find favour with those from other countries who are intrigued by Jamaica. It will be particularly heartwarming to the large Jamaican Diaspora scattered throughout the world, many of whom lived similar carefree childhoods.

The stories chart experiences that are of a middle-class boy of diverse parentage growing up in a period that straddled political independence. It is a Tom Sawyer-esque tale of life silhouetted against a society that had pockets of wealth but was largely one of abject poverty in a small country that had suffered the grossest abuses of slavery, yet it had a surprisingly strong tolerance for race, religion and class.

My parents were as diverse as the society. My dad was from a rural, protestant, mixed Scottish/ English/Welsh family that had in-country roots stretching back to the early post-slavery period. He was an intellectual with a hard-won university education in a country that had not yet fully embraced the need for education. On the other hand my mother was from first generation French and Irish Roman Catholic parents who arrived in Jamaica in the 1890's, favoured large families, embraced the Church and was possessing of a deep social tolerance.

Returning to Jamaica in 1935 from a depression-ravaged New York, my dad put his business skills, learnt at Bloomingdales Department Store and Columbia University, to work in the business of a Lebanese-Jamaican family. But that proved too restrictive for a young man with a strong independence of spirit and he soon married the love of his life and moved back to the countryside, where they would raise a family of five.

The family farm, Browndale, was where my formative years unwound. It was on the western edge of the St. Catherine plains and was surrounded by a diverse rural society that was largely employed in farming, and in particular, the sugar cane economy. The society in which we grew up was a palette of many different racial groups from Africa, Asia, Europe and the Middle East that had been a virtual melting pot since the early plantation economy. The Jews had arrived as a part of the Spanish settlement of the 16th century; the French as refugees of the early 19th century slave revolution in St. Dominique (Haiti); the Dutch settlers arrived as part of the 1667 land-swap that gave the Dutch the country of Surinam in exchange for what is now Manhattan. European immigration waves started in the 1840s, with each group initially clinging to their culture for a generation or so before being swept up at the edges into the whirlpool of the melting pot, leaving smaller and smaller cores of pure blood migrant groups.

The stores in this book revolve around these groups but are not an attempt at anthropological study; more so they are observations of a youngster who struggled to find this place, seeming to fit everywhere, yet nowhere. My father's side of the family was the more interesting, with none fully accepting their place in society. Cliff, my dad's brother was a Reverend Minister in the Scottish Church; was married into the highest levels of colonial society, yet he was impishly disrespectful of that same society, instead choosing lifelong friends from more humble backgrounds. Will, the youngest, exhibited a high leisure preference from a young age; he cared little about money, fashion or his place in society. My dad was incorruptible, had a lasting belief in fairness and the betterment of oneself and shared a common bond with my mother to help people who were ambitious but lacking in means.

As newlyweds in 1940, my parents, Monica and Basil, sold most of their possessions to purchase the small farm just a few miles west of Spanish Town. Basil having grown up in rural Jamaica had a working knowledge of farming and was all too ready to become his own boss. Monica was a city girl but enthusiastically embarked on this adventure of life on a farm. They lived on this small farm for over three decades, raising and education their five children and becoming a dynamic part of this small community. Work on a dairy farm meant rising at 2 a.m., so between two and four in the afternoon Mom had her scheduled nap, the perfect window of opportunity for us to get into trouble.

The stories in this book chronicle the innocence of my childhood and hark back to a time of freedom and security seldom enjoyed by children growing up today.

Chapter one

Browndale

My dad bought Browndale, the family farm, in about 1943. After eight years working as a manager in the Issa and Myers businesses in Kingston he decided to return to his roots in the countryside to raise his growing family.

Browndale covered sixty-five acres and was located on Featherbed Lane, about two and a half miles west of Spanish Town. The name of that road was a source of constant embarrassment to us as children and must also have been some bother to a neighbour, John Valdez, as he paid a fee to the authorities in 1950 to have the name changed to Homestead Road. But the name Featherbed Lane lives on to this day.

Our neighbours were an interesting mix. At the corner of Featherbed Lane and St. John's Road sat three shops, one owned by a just-arrived Hong Kong Chinese man who spoke little English and seemed to live in complete isolation from the rest of the community, except for his sponsor, Mrs. Soon-Fah, a Spanish Town grocer. The second shop was owned by an Indian family, whose family roots went back to the 1845 when indentured labour was brought into Jamaica from southern India. The third shop was owned by a black family. The Chinese shop was always open and seemed to do a much brisker business than the others, even though it was the only one without a bar. The key to his business was to stay open on a Sunday, when you could always go to the back of the shop, knock on a wooden door and get service. Featherbed Lane also had a mix of small farms, populated by a mix of Indian and black families and further south, a few large sugar cane farms and two 'gentlemen' farms that were owned by wealthy professionals from Kingston.

Our house was originally a two-bedroom wood frame farmhouse that was raised on pillars to a height of about three feet above the surrounding land and that allowed the cooling wind to flow on all sides. The roof was made of corrugated, galvanized steel sheets known as 'zinc roof' in Jamaica. Because of the prevalence of hurricanes and the habit of this type of roofing to take flight, one always painted ones initials on the underside to aid later recovery. A more substantial third bedroom was built in 1950 when my youngest sister Mary was due to be born and was to be our lifesaver during and after the 1951 hurricane when the rest of the house was partially demolished.

The most prominent feature of the house though was the large lattice-enclosed wrap-around verandah. The verandah was 'L' shaped and sat on the north-eastern corner of the house. This room was the entertainment area, and it was here that our parents entertained the constant stream of friends and relatives that visited each week.

The kitchen was detached to keep the wood smoke from the cast-iron Caledonia stove away from the house. The garage was a separate building and to the rear of the garage was a block of rooms that were for the use of the farm and its workers.

In later years Uncle Frankie, our mom's youngest brother came to live with us and dad bought a one-room worker's cottage from a nearby sugar estate and had it moved in one piece and erected on pillars, next to the main house. Our dear uncle Frankie was gay and this was a concern to the townspeople who unnecessarily feared for our welfare. The Jamaican society was, and still is, a very homophobic society and the presence of a gay man within a family of young boys caused such a strong reaction among the townspeople that a delegation of the town leadership came out to the farm out of concern for our welfare. My dad thanked them for their concern and told them that he was aware of the danger as he ushered them out the front door. My mom protected her younger brother fiercely and my dad was a very tolerant man; Uncle Frankie really was not a bother, being of a very un-threatening and likeable nature.

The lawn area between the house and Featherbed Lane, about an acre, was crossed by two irrigation ditches and was well populated by large guango and thorny acacia trees. The guango (known as the Saman tree in Trinidad) is similar in spread to the Live Oak of the American south and could get huge, with branches that would grow parallel to the ground for long distances. Cattle farmers prized these trees for their shade and for the generous crops of edible purple-black pods that they would bear each year. However, they were the first victims of hurricanes. The acacia were reminiscent of those on the Kenya plains, very thorny with feathery leaves and an umbrella shape. The thorns would dry out and fall to the ground, making life miserable to the bare foot. The common name for these trees was 'cashaw'.

A large, leaning guango tree to the northeast of the house held our tree house, a rude arrangement of scrap board. For those less nimble we built rungs by nailing strips of wood to the trunk. The nails would eventually work their way out and would have to be reattached while the tree oozed copious amounts of gum to seal the wound. About twelve feet up, the tree put out horizontal branches and it was in a 'Y' fork of one of these large branches, about fifteen feet out from the trunk, that we built our fort. The construction was crude with rough pieces of lumber nailed across the crotch. Getting out there from the trunk was the test, though, as one had to walk along the top of a 9-inch wide branch with no hand support.

It was in this setting that the five children, Geraldine, Christopher, Paul, Rosalind and Mary lived out a charmed and happy childhood.

The People Working at Browndale

We always had household staff. There was a cook, a washer and, when we were young, nannies. Although we were not wealthy, it was an unwritten social contract that the 'rich' people would always hire a few poorer people in the area. My mom helped many of these to migrate to find better jobs and we never saw it as serfdom, as some now make it out to be. Now this is not to say that there were no abuses, and in the island for at least one hundred years a true type of serfdom named the 'school girl' system existed. How this was supposed to work was that a very poor family with a daughter who they could not support would send her to live and work with a family that was better off. It was understood that the girl would do chores in return for food, clothing, shelter and some basic schooling (hence the term school girl). What often happened, though, was everything except the schooling was done, and many of these girls were abused sexually by the man and boys of the house.

Etty, my nanny, was the daughter of a neighbour, Mr. Nairn, though she soon migrated with her husband Mel and daughter Vandolyn to England. They joined a wave of migration of poor Jamaicans into England starting in about 1950 that was to grow to a flood during that decade. The mode of travel was by ship and the one-way fare was advertised frequently in *The Daily Gleaner* at seventy-five pounds. At an average salary of one pound ten shillings per week, it must have been difficult to accumulate this fare, but my mother always encouraged and actively helped anyone who showed some desire to improve their lives and she was responsible for the migration of at least ten families. Etty's family was one of the success stories, and on a visit to London in 1964 my parents met with Mel who was then a taxi driver and he gave them a grand tour of the city. Their daughter had become a professional athlete and had represented Britain as a 100-meter hurdler.

Daphne and Lester

"Lord God busha, come quick! Lester chop up Daphne and hang 'imself!" The day was just dawning one crisp December morning and marked a watershed in my life. First light that day seemed to bring a dawning of a deeper understanding of the strife of life, of hate and love, the social gaps and the awareness of race in pre-independent Jamaica. This was to be one incident that marked all of us children with horror that was outside of normal life experiences.

Farm life had its share of life and death. Calves were born daily and the bull calves, having no real utility on a dairy farm, were immediately sold to the butcher, as were older cows, worn out by life and no longer capable of economic return. The chicken we would eat at Sunday lunch would be walking around on the Saturday, meeting its end the next morning via the cutlass. My dog, Andy was accidentally run over and however hard I prayed for this awful, awful incident to be reversed, he never recovered. We shot birds and caught fish. Our ducks were sold to the Chinese merchants in Spanish Town, with a pre-determined end, thinly sliced with plum sauce. None of this prepared us, though, for the mortality of a human being to whom we had been so close.

Daphne was our cook, a tall woman with an engaging personality. She would entertain us children with stories of growing up in the Black River valley of St. Elizabeth, about eighty miles west of our home, in a town with the biblical-sounding name of Siloah. The Black River was a part of everyday life there and she would tell us of a childhood spent fishing and playing in the river: despite the social gulf between us, this was not too different from our own upbringing. She recounted how on the day before the Kendal Train crash of '57 her mother had seen a coffin-shaped cloud, and confidently predicted a disaster with the loss of two hundred lives. She was God-fearing but with a streak of superstition, mixing Christianity quite comfortably with Pokomania, an African-based religion. She had relatives among the Maroons of Northern St. Elizabeth, and she would recount tales of Accompong,

"The Land of Look Behind" and the district of "Me No Sen You No Come." This is a hard mountainous land where the Maroons, escaped slaves who had fought the English army to a standstill, were granted peace and their own Government in the late 1700s. In an area of riverless limestone known as Cockpit Country, it is a land of high rainfall and dense forests. At that time, there were no roads crossing this wild countryside; just a single-track railway. It was spectacular country. The land, strangely, did not harden its people.

Lester on the other hand was a short, jovial character; a farm worker who grew up close to our farm. His tales were of fishing for large tarpon while avoiding crocodiles. He told of landing hundred pound tarpon and of fifteen-foot crocodiles that were taking cows from the Heartlands property. He was a good worker and had been with us for about five years before striking up a relationship with Daphne. Dad did not allow cohabitation in the workers quarters, so in 1960 Lester and Daphne moved to a tenement yard on Job Lane, just a few yards away from the crossroads shop where Lester bought the rope.

Their relationship seemed normal with both individuals being fairly even tempered, but in late 1961 we got word that Daphne was going to move back to the worker's quarters on the property. There was nothing unusual about this, as common law relationships were always shifting. The pattern of these relationships was that a man would leave a relationship unless he was given a child, who would then be the reason to 'mind' (support) the mother and child. The tragedy was that many of these women saw no alternative to this unstable arrangement and ended up having too many children, all for different men. Daphne was either careful or fortunate to not become pregnant in the year of their relationship so she was unencumbered in her attempt to leave Lester. Or so she thought.

It was about five that fateful morning when we heard the awful wailing of the villagers. I was fifteen at the time and filled with the strange juxtaposing of all the fears of my own mortality and the indestructibility of youth. I was numb, and in the normal response to tragedies that the mind could not immediately comprehend, did not believe that something so horrible could have happened. We children were told to stay at home and dad walked up the road with his shotgun – I have no idea why he carried it with him. The ambulance took Daphne away to an uncertain fate.

She had started to carry out her plan to move from the tenement and was on the very first trip down the front step with all of her crockery and small possessions in a basket on her head. Lester had earlier bought a rope and tied it to a tree and was waiting in ambush armed with a cane bill (a short, heavy sugar cane cutlass). The first chop was obviously aimed at her throat but caught the left triceps of the arm holding the basket. The second blow was higher and caught her in the mouth as her arm fell, and this cut from ear to ear, doing remarkably minor injury. He followed up with about seven more chops as she writhed screaming on the ground. She was cut all over her body and as the villagers ran to her assistance Lester climbed the tree and hanged himself.

Careful though his preparation was, he had not sharpened the cane bill and this is what saved Daphne's life. She spent a month in hospital and emerged with horrible raised scars that would stay with her for life. She returned to work with us after some six months recovery with her family in Siloah then promptly formed a relationship with another farm hand, an Indian named Donald. One would have thought that her ugly wounds and the lingering stigma of the attack would have made people stay clear of her but Daphne's personality outweighed these physical handicaps. Donald and Daphne lived together in a 'yard' and had three children over the next five years. On an additional tragic note, their youngest child drowned in the irrigation canal at about age two.

Lester was buried in the pauper's cemetery in Spanish town and for years the tale of his evil deed echoed through the small community. Most saw it as pure evil, but those of us who knew Lester could not see that evil in him. Was this a case of the jilted lover deciding to end it all in a fit of jealousy? Or was it that life on the farm hardens some to the point where a human life is as cheap as an animal's? As middle-class youngsters our upbringing made us see these on-and-off common law relationships among our poorer neighbours as essentially impermanent, not based in love but on physical need and somehow different from relationships among the middle and upper classes. With the wisdom of retrospect and many years of life experiences, I now see that there is no difference and that all relationships are fraught with the same savagery, tenderness, hopes, fears and expectations. Poverty simply limits one's options.

Chapter two

Earlier Generations

My Father's Family

M y dad, Basil, was the third of seven children born in Christiana in central Jamaica to Luther Theophilus Wilberforce (known as 'Teach') and Mary Elizabeth Virtue, known affectionately to all as 'Mistress'. Dad was born in 1902; he was preceded by Dorothy (Dot) and Helen (Nell), and followed by Clifton (Cliff), Sybil (Cis), Alan and Hugh (Will).

He attended primary school at his father's side and it must have been fairly tough, as the child was not spared the rod in that generation. Later, in about 1916, the family moved to Maryland, Hanover where Teach was named headmaster at the local one-room primary school. He and the family moved into the headmaster's cottage. I later saw this cottage, and with no more than three bedrooms was a challenging fit for a family of nine. This was very hilly country and the house sat on a slope below the main road, beside the Barnett River and not far from the schoolhouse. It was difficult to raise such a large family on a headmaster's salary so Teach bought some land for cultivation and used the crops (mostly pimento, sugar cane and later Lucea yam, a large tuber) to supplement his income. He spent a year in Cuba teaching English to further supplement his income during this period but quickly returned when he heard of the difficulties his family had in his absence.

During the building of the Panama Canal there was great demand for 'ground produce', consisting mostly of yam, to feed the large West Indian labour force and the steep hillsides were pressed into use all over Jamaica to grow these crops. Jamaica was on the direct shipping route from the USA to Panama and schooners would stop in to stock up at the wharf at Mosquito Cove, a few miles away. The legacy of growing yams was severe hillside erosion, especially in the geologically unstable sedimentary soil of Hanover, and in later years bamboo was planted in an attempt to stabilize the hillside. Bamboo soon invaded these hillsides and remains to this day.

After primary school, where he excelled, (showing a particular flair for math) dad moved to Kingston to attend Teachers' College and in about 1922 was employed as a teacher at Jamaica College (JC), a boy's boarding school for the sons of the local gentry. He was only the second Jamaican allowed to teach at JC, which was one of two schools for the sons of the upper class, the other being Munro College. The Jamaican school system was fashioned after the British system and was not meant to educate all the children equally; it was established to segregate those who would be the officers in the British army, the professional class and the senior civil servants from the workers. The vast majority of children attended only primary school or no school at all. Their lot in life was to toil as agricultural workers producing cheap commodities just like the working man in England prior to World War II.

If one looks back at this period in Jamaica, someone like my dad had very limited career options, which included becoming a teacher, a parson, a farmer (generally on less than one hundred acres of land) or a minor civil servant. That was simply the way things were back then. There were few exceptions; not even education could move you from your caste. Years later my very perceptive cousin Stephen suggested that the Virtue men were in fact non-conformists who did not accept the status quo; all of them eventually sought self-employment later in life, creating careers for themselves outside of the few thought acceptable for them. I now believe this, and see myself the same way.

In 1929, dad decided to migrate to New York to study at Columbia University. He would have to work his way through, coincidentally arriving in New York at the start of the Great Depression. He scrambled around the city for some time before landing a job at Bloomingdale's Department Store, and to supplement his income he became a private tutor for rich kids in Connecticut. This was just after the Lindbergh baby kidnapping and many wealthy families, fearing kidnapping, elected to hire private tutors for their children. He would take the train from New York to home-school boys in math and did so for five years. One of his students turned out to be brilliant at math and went on to become a USA chess champion before taking his life while at Harvard University. This was to leave a lasting impression on my father. Dad lived in the Bronx and many years later, he took my mom to see his former home which by that time had become a slum. He lived in New York until about 1935, and returned home without finishing college.

Upon returning to Jamaica and after a few weeks at his parents' home, Sunnyville, dad moved to Kingston and moved in with his brother, Will, with whom he would stay for five years. During the period between 1935 and 1940 when dad lived in Kingston he initially took a job with a Mr. Abe Issa, later to be called 'Mr. Jamaica' for his role in establishing Jamaica as a major tourist destination. Mr. Issa was a Lebanese Christian whose family had migrated earlier to Jamaica and, in addition to his business interests in Jamaica, was active in Palestinian affairs in the Middle East. Dad was given a middle management job and in 1937 was left to hold down the fort while Mr. Issa was visiting Palestine. The staff, accustomed to Mr. Issa's style of management, was uncomfortable with this new college boy, and became intransigent, precipitating his resignation. He ended up finding work with a Mr. Myers of Myers Rum, where he met and began courting my mom, Monica.

Dad had no car but had amorous intentions and would often borrow his brother's Austin 8 to take Monica out on dates. On one fateful weekend drive in the mountains, he crashed the car much to the chagrin of Will, who as a dashing gambler-bachelor was lost without his wheels. The car was taken to the dealer, a Mr. John Crook (how about that name for a car dealer!) and after it was repaired dad picked it up and promptly backed it into a passing car.

Will was the youngest son, and the only one my grandparents could afford to send to a secondary school, in this case Cornwall College in Montego Bay. He later became the chemistry teacher at the Government-owned Farm School (now the College of Agriculture, Science and Education). Will, and other members of the family, had gone to great lengths to get this job. He first landed the job on his own but had it withdrawn because his predecessor, N.W. Manley (who later became Prime Minister) had accepted an athletic scholarship in England and left his teaching position at the Farm School – apparently the Colonial Secretary (the chief representative of the Crown in the Civil Service) did not want another athlete to run out on the job, and Will was a consummate athlete. With the help of Sir Thomas Roxburgh, a prominent figure in colonial Jamaica whose granddaughter, Mabel, had married his older brother Cliff, Will was able to land the job at Farm School. Cliff interceded with Sir Thomas (strongly rumoured to be the son of King Edward VII), who then ordered the Colonial Secretary, a Mr. Brassington, to reverse the decision. Sir Thomas would have been in his late 60's by this time and, though diminutive in stature, would have been a formidable opponent. He was a titled Englishman and a highly ranked government official; colonial Jamaica was part of his domain. The Duke of York, one of King Edward's sons, was a not infrequent visitor to Annandale, the Roxburgh estate in the parish of St. Ann.

Sir Thomas's power and influence were to first hurt and then aid the marriage of Cliff and Mabel. Cliff was from the working class and was not seen as a suitable mate for Mabel. The young couple was banished when Sir Thomas revoked his job at the local Parish Council and had Cliff removed from his post as a parson in the Presbyterian Church. The young couple had no choice but to move in with Teach and Mistress since there was no job and no money. A few years later when it was apparent that this tactic had failed and that there was now a child, Sir Thomas dispatched his grandson, Frank, to check out this new family. Frank anointed the family 'poor but solid' and Cliff was returned to his old job and parsonage. He was to live out his years as an excellent, though earthy, minister at the manse at Chalky Hill. He died in 1974 and was buried at his old church at Lauriston, near Chalky Hill.

In 1935 Dad and Uncle Will leased land in Riversdale St. Catherine, and established a banana farm that became riotously productive. The problem was that dad seemed to have done all the work while Will would occasionally show up with his car filled with girls to show off his estate. The farm did well for a while but was destroyed by a hurricane in 1937; even though the hurricane never really hit Jamaica with heavy winds, it was persistent and the rain and gustiness was all that was needed. Will married a year or so before dad, and in October 1940 my parents got married in Kingston.

The desire to be self-employed drove dad to again try farming and through thrift he was able to make a small down payment in about 1943, securing the ownership of Browndale. When Alan Shaw Campbell, the estate manager for the nearby Innswood sugar plantation heard of the purchase he told dad that it was a mistake, since he had looked at Browndale and had rejected it because the land was 'bruk-ass clay'. These sixty-five acres were to feed, clothe and school the five Virtue children.

The property was sold in 1968 to a housing developer with the hope that the land would eventually be rezoned to allow housing development. This was not to happen and it was used as pasture for racehorses and was eventually converted into a poultry farm. As you drive by now, you can see that the house no longer exists and the front yard, which was once so well groomed, has been reclaimed by Mother Nature. The big guango tree is still at the gate. Few landmarks to which one can tie memories are visible and the place that was at the centre of our world is now just a memory.

My Mother's Family

My mother was born Monica Kelly in 1914 to Charles Claire Kelly and Geraldine Kelly, the fourth child in a strict Roman Catholic family that was eventually to grow to eleven, with nine girls and two boys.

Charles Claire Kelly hailed from County Cork in Ireland and was born in 1872 to Colonel Patrick Kelly and Rose Kelly. He was one of nine children. Col. Kelly was attached to an Irish regiment of the British army, and while stationed in Dover in the 1880s, his wife Rose was killed while crossing the road, run over by a horse-drawn cart. Charles was at that time a difficult child and with the loss of a very doting mother, Col. Kelly decided that Charles and his siblings should attend a Catholic boarding school in Belgium. Charles, though embittered by his forced separation from his father, found great comfort in his siblings and graduated with excellent grades. He was to remain very close with all his siblings even into old age and kept up a lively correspondence with them until his death in 1952.

My great-grandfather's regiment was subsequently garrisoned in Jamaica, and during this time he decided that Charles should become a navy man. After leaving convent school Charles joined the British Navy at age seventeen at the lowest officer rank of Officer Cadet. It was a hard life, and after a few years Charles chafed at the discipline and rigor of the life. The resentment of Navy discipline was joined by a dread of the ocean after a horrendous voyage through the Magellan Straits in 1891 that nearly cost him his life, after which he vowed to leave the service. Charles resigned his commission as soon as he could and joined his father in Kingston.

History does not record what type of reception this renegade got from his father when he arrived in Jamaica, but it is known that Charles settled down and joined the Jamaican civil service, retiring in the mid-1930's as the island's Auditor General. In his early days in Jamaica he was reputed to be a man-about-town with many female companions but he was smitten by the young Geraldine Crosswell and they married in 1907. He was at that time thirty four years old and she was eighteen.

Abraham Crosswell, Geraldine's grandfather, was born in 1804 in Bern, Switzerland. He was a professor at the local university and a strong supporter of the ideals of Baruch Spinoza, the seventeenth century Dutch philosopher. Though he was a university professor, his Jewish faith and strange Spinoza philosophy kept him at the margins of society and in 1837 he migrated to Jamaica. He soon involved himself in politics and three decades later he earned the wrath of the British Governor, Edward Eyre, when he supported his friend George William Gordon who was accused of involvement in an uprising of poor black Jamaicans called the Morant Bay Rebellion. George William Gordon was executed, and Abraham and family were expelled from Jamaica in late 1867. Soon after this, he showed up in the United States, after a short stay with friends in Santiago, Cuba.

Abraham, as was his nature, again became involved in civic affairs in the small city of New Orleans. Recognized by the US Federal Government for his great civic work during a yellow fever outbreak, he was appointed Consul of the US Embassy in Haiti. His two sons had in the meantime married and settled in Haiti and Jamaica. My grandmother Geraldine was one of five children born in Haiti to Noel Crosswell, Abraham's second son. Abraham retired from the US State Department in about 1873, moved back to Jamaica and died in Kingston in 1876.

Geraldine had had an interesting life by the time she married. She was orphaned at the age of fourteen when her father, a pharmacist living in Haiti, got involved in local politics and was said to have been poisoned at the Haitian President's instructions. Geraldine's mother had earlier died and she and her younger sister, Tita, were sent to live with friends and relatives outside Haiti. Geraldine went to Santiago, Cuba to live with the American Consul General's family there. Tita was sent to live in Rae Town, Jamaica as a companion to a Jewish family. After two years in Cuba, Geraldine was sent to live with an uncle in Jamaica. Arriving in about 1904 at the age of fifteen, she found her younger sister living in absolute squalor in Rae Town and had her move in with her.

Grandpa Charles Kelly was sixteen years older than his wife Geraldine and ruled his household with an iron hand. He had lost his Catholic faith in his carousing years but held on to enough of it that he insisted that Geraldine convert to Catholicism prior to the marriage. It took the great earthquake of January 14, 1907 to reacquaint him with the church and every morning thereafter he could be seen walking down North Street to Holy Trinity cathedral, dressed in full white. The earthquake and the fire that followed were devastating to the city of Kingston, killing eight hundred individuals. Charles barely escaped with his life when the walls of his second floor office on Harbour Street fell outwards taking the roof to one side. He was left sitting at his desk covered in dust and looking at the sky. His personal miracle and the survival of his young girlfriend were to trigger a religious recidivism that would see him fully re-embrace his former Catholic faith. He spent the next two weeks helping burn the bodies dug from the ruins and this built a crust on his personality that was to remain to his death. That cataclysm was preceded by the great San Francisco earthquake in 1906 and followed by the great Messina earthquake in 1908. Clustered in the same decade were volcanic eruptions in Martinique, St. Vincent and Sicily and earthquakes in Venezuela, Nicaragua and Chile. These were apparently compelling evidence of a wrathful God and Charlie paid heed.

Geraldine survived the earthquake by sheer luck – she happened to be outdoors when the house where she was boarding collapsed in a pile of bricks. They married nine months later, in October 1907, in the chapel at Alpha Convent, one of the few places of religion that survived the earthquake.

Those were difficult times but the Kelly's started a family that was to grow to eleven children by 1924. All their children went to Catholic school – the girls to Alpha Convent and the boys to St. George's College. Although he had a good government post as Auditor General, Charles was unable to afford this expense without supplemental income and he started a grape orchard at his Kingston Gardens residence. The vines were so prolific that they earned enough to allow the family a comfortable middle class lifestyle. Of all the children, only my mother, Monica, her sister Claire and brother Joseph married Jamaicans. The girls met American and British servicemen during the war and most married and moved to their husband's countries.

The young Monica Kelly was employed at Myers Rum Company where she met her future husband, a 36-year-old confirmed bachelor who was immediately smitten. My maternal grandfather was fiercely protective of his progeny and had to sign off on the many suitors of his nine pretty daughters. He would chase away many a prospect with the words "I don't want any penny-farthing boy visiting my daughter!" Apparently dad was a hit; being in his late 30's must have worked to his advantage as he would have been more a contemporary of Charlie than the others.

Charles Claire Kelly's strict discipline, crustiness and the marital age gap led in the late 1940s to his eviction by Geraldine from the family home to a singular existence in a rooming house. My grandmother had never had a chance to enjoy her youth and, armed with a small inheritance, she took advantage of the period after the war to buy her own house on Roosevelt Avenue in Kingston. She maintained a full travel schedule visiting her numerous children. Later, her base was our home on Featherbed Lane and she lived with us there from about 1957 until her death in 1961.

My mom, Monica, was the strongest personality of her siblings and was the only one who would confront her father when she believed he was being too heavy-handed or when she disagreed with him on issues. She had a fierce belief that girls should be as well educated as boys and was persistent in her efforts to ensure that all our cousins were held to this standard. She was disappointed if they did not follow her ideals. This dream extended not just to the family but also to the workers at our farm and the people in our district. She personally helped many migrate to England during the 1950s and kept in touch with them to see that they settled in well. She hated sloth and laziness.

She never fully adjusted to country life after moving to Browndale in 1943, missing her friends and family in Kingston. She hated the mosquitoes and the swamp and the apparent callousness handed down to animals that was a part of farming life – she particularly hated the fact that old cows that were no longer able to produce sufficient quantities of milk were sold to butchers with little regard for their years of valuable service. To ease the loneliness of country life, she arranged for friends to visit from Kingston every Wednesday night and formed lasting friendships with families nearby. My dad was conscious of her dislike for country life and made sure that we spent most weekends with my grandmother in Kingston.

Though of a nervous nature, she never transferred this to her children. We were all allowed a surprising level of freedom to roam the countryside and all developed an independence of being and a love for travel and seeing new places.

Sunnyville

My earliest memory of Sunnyville, my paternal grandparents' property in the parish of Hanover in northwest Jamaica, was Christmas of 1951. We arrived late in the evening after a long drive from Spanish Town in my dad's Ford. The long, steep driveway was not negotiable by most cars and we got as far as the dreaded yellow plum tree before the wheels spun on the wet grass and we had to stop. We climbed the last 150 yards or so up to the house where we were met by an always-smiling Grandma. Grandpa Luther Virtue built the house at Sunnyville in about 1935 on property he had bought in 1930. Sunnyville was part of the old slave-era New Retrieve property that had long since failed as a sugar cane plantation and had been subdivided and sold off to pay debts. Teach was close to retirement age when he built the house. At about the same time, his second son Cliff had married Mabel Roxburgh and needed a home, so Sunnyville met both their needs.

His choice of a site must have seemed strange to the locals. The property was actually a seventy-acre conical hill that rose to about eight hundred feet above sea level. It had a stream, New Works, which rose on the western side and ran counter clockwise around the southern and eastern sides, exiting to the north into Mosquito Cove. People in Hanover did not build on hilltops because of the difficulty of getting water from the streams that would have been hundreds of feet below in the valleys. Grandpa came from Christiana in central Jamaica where there were no streams and so everybody there had a rainwater tank. Sunnyville had a large open tank, perhaps seventeen feet deep, which was fed by a gutter system with water from the zinc roof. This part of Jamaica had about one hundred inches of rain a year and water was never a problem, except that you had to use a bucket and rope to dip water from the tank. Many of my recollections of early childhood are associated with smells and tastes, and my memory of the drinking water, which was always boiled and stored in an earthenware jug, is of a slightly metallic taste.

The construction was wood frame, using hand-sawn timbers from the property. One thing I always found odd was that the wall was only complete on the outside – the inside wall showed the 2"x 4" studs, though it was nicely painted. The verandah was about twelve feet wide and swept around the western, northern and eastern sides of the house with sweeping panoramic views on all three sides. It was elevated on a foundation about five feet high and had the typical zinc roof.

The view of Mosquito Cove from the north side of the house was exceptional. Mosquito Cove is shaped like a miniature Lake Michigan. It had been the busiest port in Jamaica while the Panama Canal was being built, with sailing schooners calling for loads of Lucea, Renta, Yellow, Negro and Afu yams that had been grown on the surrounding hillsides for the West Indian workers in Panama. Farmers would dig yam hills on the steep slopes in the area, and the abundance of bamboo in the area was probably the result of its use as terracing for the turn-of-the-century yam plantations. The town and port of Lucea was visible to the northwest, but even then it was of dwindling importance as the small sugar mills in the area surrendered to low sugar prices. Dolphin Head Mountain range with its craggy profile vaguely resembling that of a dolphin dominated the south western distance.

A small room on the north side was the larder since there was no electricity and only a small kerosene-fuelled refrigerator. This was where all the 'ground provisions', such as yams, yampie and other tubers were stored. The room was always filled with a strange combination of smells – coffee mixed with pimento and other unknown aromas. During the pimento picking season the verandah would double as a place to hand-strip the green pimento berries from the twigs that had been broken from the trees by the reapers – it was common belief that a tree had to be fairly heavily pruned to sustain a good crop. The heaps of leaves were warm, even hot, to the touch (perhaps through fermentation) and on the chilly winter days when temperatures hovered in the low 60's, it was nice to burrow under the leaves, as children would. From about 1952 until 1956, several grandchildren would be shipped off to Sunnyville to spend summers with Mistress, and we would help with the pimento harvest as part of our chores. Mistress, my cousins (Dawne, Marcia, Geraldine, Rosy, Steve, Chris and Audrey) and I would sit squat-legged in piles of pimento twigs. We would pull each branch through a closed hand and strip off the small green berries. The occasional ripe berries were bright purple and those would be eaten or put aside to make a liqueur.

Although Sunnyville's elevation was modest, the temperatures were somewhat cooler than average, usually in the 70's and low 80's, but I recall around Christmas time one year when a 'Norther' was blowing that the wind moaned through the night and temperatures fell to what must have been the low 60's. 'Northers' were cold fronts that would blow down from the American continent each winter, accompanied by strong north winds that could clock over sixty miles per hour. This was the only time the north-facing shoreline would encounter the surf, and it meant rough seas and wet, cold days and nights. This phenomenon was a danger to the banana industry and led scientists to develop trees that were shorter and stronger. At Sunnyville it meant bundling up time.

The property was fruitful. A Number-eleven and a Turpentine mango tree grew close to the main gate, near the spring that formed the

New Works River. The yellow plum tree was a prolific bearer. There was a grove of the sweetest tangerines to the northwest of the house and in the front yard were a huge Bombay mango tree, a guinep tree and a custard apple tree. All of them were riddled with worms, but this wasn't a problem for us children; we would simply nibble around the wrigglers. Next to the outhouse on the eastern side was an alligator pear tree (a long necked avocado). Pimento trees and the odd breadfruit tree grew everywhere. There was a line of Flame of the Forest trees lining the last hundred yards of the driveway – large trees with brilliant scarlet cockscomb flowers that would unfurl from canoe-shaped pods. In full bloom, a hillside of these trees was almost as memorable as the Immortelle trees of Trinidad.

Also on the property, next to a small waterfall, was the wreckage of a sturdy stone building that we called 'The Works'. It had once housed a water mill that had been used for crushing and processing sugar cane. The machinery of sugar manufacturing was still strewn about – the large iron kettles resembling British soldier's WW1 helmets, a Chattanooga mill that had been used to crush the cane after the water mill fell into disrepair and the remnants of an old water wheel.

The New Works stream scoured out the jet-black rocks of the riverbed into a series of small falls and open pools. It teemed with small fish, probably mullet, and various varieties of small crabs and shrimp. We spent many happy hours turning rocks over in search of crustaceans, though at the end of play none of us looked forward to the very steep hike back to the house. Those were happy times. Pre-teen boy and girl cousins mixed without fighting and would wander, mostly completely unsupervised, to explore the countryside.

Mistress shared with mom an aggravated fear of lightning and she could not have chosen a worse place to live than Sunnyville. The house was just below the typical thunderstorm cloud base, and storms were numerous and vicious. My dad once told us that one afternoon while sitting on the verandah, he had seen lightning strike a coconut tree just feet away, so close he was showered with pieces of bark. While the endless violent summer afternoon thunderstorms swirled around us, we would read old volumes of Encyclopaedia Britannica under the house, doubtless left over from Teach's headmaster days,

For indoor entertainment, we would make shadow-shapes on the walls using the light from the kerosene lamps, and occasionally listen to the car battery-powered Grundig radio. The battery had to be regularly recharged and, with no family car, I suspect that my grandparents only used the radio to listen to the BBC news except when one of their sons was visiting and could take the battery for recharging. The radio was one of those pre-World War II models, huge, with a wooden case and a transparent frequency-chart which showed the names of cities with radio stations – London, Berlin, Budapest, New York, Rio. We knew every station and through city names were able to learn the capitals of most of the world's countries by looking them up in Britannica.

Summer days meant the beach. Bull Bay was a small half moon of white sand about five miles west of Lucea that was protected from the prevailing north-west wind by a rocky headland. The honeycombed rock of the headland was prime exploration ground and it was riddled with shallow solution holes, caves and a spectacular blowhole. The sea on the outside of the headland had no reef and the deep-water swells would pound the rock, filling the underwater caves to overflowing onto the surface. The next wave would arrive as the overflow was draining and the compressed air that it pumped into the cave would shoot water thirty feet into the air. It was not unusual to spot large fish from the rocks, usually Blue Parrot in the ten pound range. These grazers of the reef would constantly nip at the moss that grew on the reef and we were told that they were responsible for creating the sand on the beach. Bull Bay itself was calm, glass-clear water with small coral heads and a sandy bottom. We would dive down with goggles and seek out the small fish, all of which had spectacular colours, hiding under the ledges in the coral. My recollection is of endless sunburn and a ravening hunger that can only come after a day at the beach.

On the way back to Sunnyville we would drive by small bays where fishermen would be landing with their day's catch, and from time to time we would see fishermen lugging baskets across the road loaded with dolphin(Mahi Mahi), kingfish, snapper and even the odd tuna. Uncle Cliff once told us of a fish he saw in Lucea market that weighed over 400 pounds (probably a Blue Fin Tuna). The tail was missing – taken by sharks as the fisherman was landing it with a hand line from a twelve-foot dugout canoe. The fishermen, because of the cost, almost never used fishing rods. In fact, these were the days before widespread use of nylon line when most fishing line was made of braided cotton. It must have been hell on the hands.

Close to Lucea we would pass Fort Charlotte, guarding the approach to Lucea Harbour. The fort sat on a 30 foot cliff on the western approach to the harbour and still had large cannon mounted in turrets. Tracked incline rails were used to slide the larger weapons into shooting positions above the wall then roll them back to be muzzle loaded on the esplanade area behind the wall. The fort had been converted into the local parish road works headquarters, since pirates and the French were in decline. Years before, my dad's sister, Aunt Cis, had lived at Fort Charlotte where her husband, Uncle Herbert, had been the Parish Council works manager. At the base of the cliff, the sea was about twenty to forty feet deep and it contained many pilot fish and barracuda; Aunt Cis used to tell of the grizzled old tiger shark that would show up each evening, in those days when the garbage was thrown over the wall.

Rusea's School campus was next to the fort. Founded in the early 1800's, Aunt Cis and Uncle Cliff had both attended school there. It was built in the same architectural style as the fort with cut-stone arches supporting a large rectangular building that was elevated to catch the ever-present trade winds through green jalousie windows. The land sloped away to the north to a whitecap freckled, restless sea of the most brilliant blue and purple.

In Lucea we would stop at a bakery and dad would buy 'grotto' and 'bulla'. Still eaten in Jamaica today, grotto is a white hard-shelled biscuit that was about six inches round and in retrospect was quite tasteless, much like any hard biscuit. Dad told us that grotto originated from hardtack which served as a staple on sailing ships of earlier centuries, where its ability to avoid spoilage was legendary. Bulla was a small, round cake, a baked mixture of flour and molasses, retaining some moisture in its heavy taste. We enjoyed these occasional snacks, these staples of the poor, and looked forward to the stop at the bakery.

Some Sundays we would drive up a steep driveway to visit an old Presbyterian parson named Rev. John Rothney. The Rothneys had arrived from Aberdeen many decades earlier and he was about ninety years old (or so it seemed), but was a kindly old Scottish gentleman who always had sweets for the kids. The parsonage was on a bluff overlooking the harbour and had the most spectacular view. We kids would romp on the lawn while our parents visited.

The drive back to Jericho, the village near Sunnyville, was up a steep, unpaved road. The car would just barely make the last few yards up the road, chugging through the last steep corner. The Sunday church service would just be emptying out, and we would often be recognized by the older villagers, many of whom were my father's contemporaries. They had all sat in the same one-room school with Teach as the local headmaster. The country people of Jamaica were most colourful on Sundays. Everybody wore their 'Sunday best' clothes, with men in jackets, women in violet or white dresses and the children well scrubbed and grudgingly in tow. The local bakery was the only store in town open on Sunday (though there were probably only three shops in all), and I will always remember the smell of fresh bread. Somehow, and perhaps it is because we were young and unaware, the country people back then seemed happier with fewer possessions than modern people are accustomed to.

It was March of 1954 when Teach died. He had been nursing a hernia for some years, and as it got worse he decided to go to the doctor in Lucea. He had arranged to have a car meet him at the foot of Sunnyville hill as he did not have one of his own, but it did not show up and he attempted to walk to Jericho in the pouring rain. He died later that week of peritonitis, brought on by a strangulated hernia that was caused by the walk. I well remember the news arriving by telegram in

Spanish Town. This was the fastest means of communication and a postman on a bicycle always delivered it – he may as well have carried a scythe, as a telegram almost always bore grim news. My mom screamed out at the news, as she did with each death in the family. Grandpa was buried later that week in the cemetery behind the Presbyterian Church in Lucea. He was eighty years old and left a widow who refused to become a burden to her children, and continued to live on at Sunnyville.

Mistress grew up in Christiana, Jamaica and married Luther Virtue in the late 1890's. They had seven children between 1898 and 1913 – an average family for the times. My dad seemed to have been the most academically gifted, and was probably a favourite because he was conscientious and hard working. His three brothers, Cliff, Alan and Will, were all athletic and Clark Gable good-looking. All had engaging and terrific personalities, and I suspect were successful suitors of many young ladies in the area.

Mistress was a sweet lady who was always cheerful, though with a streak of independence. She continued to welcome the large broods of Virtue, Walcott, Phillips and Williams grandchildren for another four years after Teach died until her own death in 1956 from an apparent heart attack. She is also buried in the Presbyterian churchyard in Lucea, next to her loving husband.

After Mistress died, the family got together and sold Sunnyville to Uncle Cliff. Cliff turned this into his retreat and for many years he would welcome the rest of the family for fishing and relaxation. He was an avid, skilled fisherman and kept a dugout canoe at Mosquito Cove, a short distance away. Uncle Cliff added running water and a bathroom and extended the verandah, making the place a lot more livable. He even paved the driveway, making passage by car a possibility. The property was able to pay its way through the revenue from pimento, and in my teen years it became a place where cousins and friends would hang out. Cousin Steve did most of his studying for his law exams there, often distracted when we would drop by with girlfriends for the weekend.

Cliff died in 1974 and I have not visited the property since. My sisters Geraldine, Rosy and Mary visited with their spouses in the mid-1980s and found a dilapidated structure. I would rather keep the memories than see it that way.

Chapter three

Making Ends Meet

*L*ife was not easy running a farm with marginal resources. It was equally as hard being one of those resources and, not coincidentally, none of the five of us children even considered following in dad's footsteps. Though I look back at these times with a certain amount of fondness, it was physically hard and socially difficult – you just try going to high school on the back of a mule-drawn milk cart!

Browndale's soil was almost all clay and true to the words of Alan Shaw Campbell of Innswood, the neighbouring sugar estate, it proved unsuitable for most crops. We tried rice, with some success; we tried sugar cane, but the labour was a problem, so Browndale ended up being mostly a dairy farm. Now it is not possible for a family of seven to survive on the income from a sixty-five acre dairy farm, so dad developed strategies for begging grazing rights in a number of creative ways. One strategy was to board out some of the herd and the other was built around foraging, but neither of these tactics was sustainable and by the late 1950s the family was forced to buy another property.

The boarding tactic sought the help of an old friend, a Mr. Caryl at Heartlands, a property about five miles away. The pregnant and young cows that did not need milking would be sent to Heartlands and when the pregnant cows were near the point where they were about to calve there would be a two-way cattle drive, moving the now 'dry' cows (not giving milk because of pregnancy or youth) from Browndale to Heartlands and returning the same day with the mature cows and those about to calve. This was a whole-day exercise and, because we had to use public roads, it was always done on a Sunday to take advantage of low traffic volumes. Cows were the most stupid creatures when it came to traffic – they would not hurry and would not stay out of the middle of the road. We would walk beside them, trying our best to keep them in a group o the side of the road. We also had to keep them away from every open gateway as they would always go in and eat anything they found. The old station wagon would drive alongside us down the dusty white marl road, with my mother, head tied with a scarf, doling out lemonade and running the operation like a basketball coach, bringing in reserve herders from the bench and resting the starters as they tired. No houseguest was overlooked in this enterprise, and although the cattle drive was torture for us, oddly enough the Kingston cousins saw it as a novelty and gladly participated. Tom Sawyer was really on to something with the fence-painting caper. The Heartlands drive stopped in 1957, when Mr. Caryl's nephew, a Kingston land developer, convinced his uncle to stop giving us access. The cooperation in the countryside of people sharing resources must have seemed odd to him.

Foraging was provided in two ways. After the neighbouring farmers had reaped their rice crops, there was always a certain amount of grass growing on the edges of the fields; allowing cows in reduced the clean up for the next crop. Dad was also able to negotiate a 'cane top' gathering agreement with Innswood Sugar Estate. The cane top is the leafy upper part of the cane plant that was discarded during harvesting and left in the fields to otherwise decay. The tops would be gathered by our workers, hauled home on mule-drawn carts and chopped up and fed to the cows in a semi-feedlot operation. The 'pickers' were almost all women, and they would collect the tops into 'cane bands' of about seven tops each and tie them with strips of leaves. They were paid by the number of bands collected, and at the end of the day they would load the mule-drawn dray and be transported home on top of a heap seven or eight feet high. The cane bands would be offloaded at the cowshed where a late nineteenth-century chaffing machine with two huge blades along the spokes of a belt-driven three-foot diameter iron wheel would be used to chop them into one-inch segments. This was almost an industrial operation, with a pulley-driven machine chopping away while one worker fed it and another shovelled away the chaff. It could remove fingers in a heartbeat. Cane tops were a valuable resource that enabled a feedlot operation that could increase the cattle population for the small acreage we had, but the estates started burning the cane fields by the late 1950s and that destroyed the tops.

One day in the late 1950s one of the pickers fell from the dray when the wheel jarred against a train track. After she fell, she complained of no feeling below the neck, a sign that her spinal cord was damaged. Eager to help, the other workers decided that she needed to be warmed with hot water. When she insisted that the water must be too cool since she could not feel it, they continued heating the water until she developed huge blisters all over her body. Mom was horrified when they arrived home and took her to hospital immediately, but it was too late and she later died of the burns.

The cows were milked at 4:00 a.m. and again at about 3:00 p.m. A cooperative named Dairy Products Ltd. was owned by dad and a number of the local farmers and it would send a truck to collect the milk churns at 7:00 a.m. and 5:00 p.m. each day. The company had a milk distributorship and an ice creamery; the milk was pasteurized and distributed each morning to Kingston doorsteps by horse-drawn wagons, using returnable glass bottles with push-in cardboard tops. The actual milking was done by hand until early 1963 when dad bought a milking machine.

The milking process involved driving twenty-four head at a time into the milk shed where two parallel rows of stalls would hold the cows. The stalls were simple, a series of vertical hardwood posts with one side swinging open at the top to allow the cow's head to enter and exit. The cow would put her head in, enticed by a trough full of coconut-meal grain and chaff, and the stanchion would be pushed shut. A wooden toggle would hold it shut, trapping the head, though most of the cows soon learnt to use their horns to push the toggle up and release the stanchion themselves.

After we had a full shed, the udders would be washed and sterilized – sometimes if they were really muddy it could take gallons of water and up to ten minutes each – then you would get a milk bucket, squat on the right side of the cow and hand-milk. The trick was to avoid four hazards: getting kicked by the cow (some had to be chained, by putting shackles behind their knees); getting kicked by the cow behind you; getting stepped on; and getting hit by a tail full of dried mud – an almost sure knockout punch. One also had to be alert to the mood of the cow. A sudden hunching motion meant the cow was about to pee or crap, and this happened often. You needed to stand up and get away, or you and the milk would be surely splashed. One had to be nimble, and a seat would just get in the way.

Each cow would give from 4 to 12 quarts (British quarts, or about 25% more than a US quart), depending on how long it had been since they had had a calf. Cows were the ultimate manipulators and could withhold favours at will. At the start, most of them would not 'send down the milk' unless you shovelled them extra grain, and you would squat there pulling away and getting nothing. Some were easy to milk and some were hard. The biggest cows had the biggest nipples and a ripple-squeeze motion would yield a steady stream. The smaller cows had small tits about the size of a finger and one had to use a stripping technique, occasionally wetting the tit with milk from the bucket, and pinching and sliding the thumb and index finger down the tit.

Milking was not a regular exercise for us boys, but often enough one or all of the milk hands would not show and dad would shake us awake, shouting "Pops [his name for me] and Chris, get up, the men have not shown up". This most often happened on a Saturday morning after the payday drink up at the local bar, and these were not pleasant words to hear. The cows simply had to be milked. The two of us would have to milk about forty cows, with multiple trips to empty the bucket into large milk churns. As each batch of cows was milked, we would drive them into the holding pen and bring in some more. This would go on for about two hours and was tough on the forearms. Ever the one to please, Chris would take charge, and he would always take on the challenge of milking the most cows and the most difficult ones. Dad would praise him for his efforts, and I, not needing the praise, would get away with doing less. After the milking we would strain the milk through a type of cheesecloth and wheel the 40-quart churns to the roadside for pickup. Then we would have breakfast. If it was a week day, we would go to school, but if it was a weekend we would have to shovel out the dung from the shed, wash it down and then drive the cows out to pasture.

Part of the property was divided into about fifteen separate fields (pastures) varying in size from about two acres to seven. The rest of the property was given over to some sugar cane for a once per year cash crop, a field that was usually set aside for growing millet or exotic grasses with names like Napier or Guatemala that would be cut as fodder with the cane tops, and the family compound. Pasture use was rotated with dad deciding which to use every couple of days. The cows would have to be herded to the selected pasture with one person leading and another behind, and because the property was long and narrow, some drives would be up to half a mile. The rainy season was the worst time for this because the lanes would be muddied by the passage of the cows and you could easily find yourself up to your knees in a mixture of mud and cow dung.

Luckily the property had irrigation, since southern St. Catherine is in the rain shadow of the mountains and gets only 35" of rain a year. The clay soil shed most of the water from the thunderstorm downpours so the pastures had to be constantly watered. The method used was flood irrigation, where shovelling away earthen dams would open up a series of feeder trenches and water would flow in, flooding the field.

We had water rights of about twenty-five cubic yards per hour and this was sufficient to keep the place in fairly green condition. One farm worker had responsibility for watering the pastures and because of their background in rice farming, it was an Indian man named Frederick that had that duty. Frederick was rail-thin and was married to a lady named Sukie, who always wore a sari, despite one hundred years since her forebears migrated to Jamaica.

Trees were allowed to grow alongside the main irrigation ditches on the borders of the property, including large guango, logwood, coconut, almond, guava, mango and the odd calabash. The guango is a large tree with a rough bark and is somewhat reminiscent of the Live Oak of the American South. After shedding all its leaves late in the winter, the guango immediately follows with fresh lime-green leaves and a mass of bottlebrush pink flowers that yield eight-inch black pods containing tamarind-sized black seeds embedded in an ample coating of molasses-sweet flesh. The cows prized this crop and were the main means of spreading seeds. Logwood is an extremely hard, thorny, slow-growing tree that was the most sought-after dyewood in the hemisphere. A whole industry sprang up in the eighteenth century chopping and preparing logwood for export. If water is dripped on exposed logwood heartwood, it instantly bleeds blood red, slowly turning to a deep purple-black. The logwood forest went into a massive bloom once per year at the end of the summer drought and the trees would be covered in bees. The small, sweet-smelling, yellow flowers produce a light honey that was as prized as the wood. Almond trees were common in the tropics and wear large leaves on umbrella-like limbs and bear a constant load of thin-fleshed yellow fruits. I would spend many a day high up in an almond tree or guava tree eating the fruits. The calabash was a smallish tree that grows large, hollow, gourd-shaped fruit with a hard rind that was often used by the poor to make eating and storage utensils. These days, local craftsmen use them to make toys and maracas, and they can be seen at any tourist trap. Our favourite uses of calabash (or goadie, as the locals called them) was to use the tree limbs to make bows (as in bow and arrow) or to make a spring-loaded bird-catching device we called a springe. A four-foot-long branch would be cut from the calabash tree and one end would be stuck firmly into the ground, a string with a noose attached to the other end and pulled taut, like a bow, and attached to a triggering device.

In the late 1950's, after the loss of grazing rights at Heartlands, combined with the loss of access to cane tops because of the new practice of burning cane, we were forced to buy a second property named Bendon. Bendon was in the Red Hills, about three miles west of Browndale on the St. Johns Road, on the way to Kitson Town and Guanaboa Vale. It was in red earth country, most often associated with bauxite (aluminium ore) in Jamaica, and it was without surface water. When we bought it, it was covered in wild growth. There was no money to clear it for pasture so dad sold the charcoal rights to local burners and gave them a time frame to cut the saplings and smaller trees with no economic value and to burn the wood to make charcoal. Charcoal was made by stacking larger, then smaller pieces of wood into a pyramid about seven feet high, covering it with earth to slow combustion, and lighting a fire at the heart. It would burn for about a week and the oxygen-starved fire would burn the more volatile parts of the wood, leaving the carbon skeleton. Dad earned a share of the coal and used the money from its sale to bring in labourers with cutlasses to clean out the remaining bushes. We were then pressed into service to paint each cut stem with a bush killer.

The fruit trees, consisting of about fifteen varieties of mango, three of naseberry (or sapodilla, the source of the sap or chicle originally used by Mr. Wrigley to make chewing gum), cashew, sweet sop and guinep were all left standing, as were the ackee and other larger trees. By 1959 we had hand-planted about fifty acres with a grass named Pangola and dad had arranged with a neighbour to receive a small supply of well water. That neighbour, Ken Rose, a student of dad's in the 1920s, was a surveyor and a racehorse owner. He had earlier bought a well digger from one of the wildcatting Americans that were constantly on the hunt for oil in the 1950s. Ken's wife was a water diviner and had picked out a spot on the adjoining property, Naseberry Grove, where they struck an underground stream.

Bendon then became the overflow for dry cattle, but it was to become our hunting grounds for fruit and birds, and for a valuable cash crop for the family. In 1960 mom decided to grow a trial patch of tomatoes and that first year put in a few rows of plants of various varieties. This worked well, and by the autumn of 1961 a full two acres were under tomato. Each plant had to be hand watered and staked, which was another use of boy-time. The problem of setting the seedlings was solved the first year by using quart-sized motor oil tins. We boys would have to retrieve hundreds of empty quart-sized oilcans from the riverbank behind Valentine gas station in Spanish Town. We would then use an old-fashioned can opener to cut off the top of each can, punch a few holes in the bottom for drainage, fill it with dirt and press in two seeds. The cans were then held in a nursery area where they were watered each day until the plants were about a foot tall, after which the root balls were shaken out of the cans and planted in rows in mom's tomato patch. The ripe tomatoes were picked and boxed, then dad would take them to Kingston and go to hotels and supermarkets in search of sales. On some occasions he would return home with unsold boxes and these would be converted (osterized, we used to say, after the brand of the blender used) into tomato juice. I still don't like tomato juice that much.

It was tough on my parents, since by that time they needed to start planning for university for us and there was a large mortgage to be paid. It wasn't until I became self-employed and had to make payroll and expenses that I appreciated the many nights they must have lain awake trying to figure out where to find the money. My parents made the down payment on Bendon by encashing all their life insurance policies, emptying their savings and ours, including even the "duck money" we had earned by growing and selling ducks, as a little side business, to the Chinese and Palestinian families in the area. Dad did not qualify for bank loans or traditional mortgages so he borrowed money from friends such as Keith Brice and the family lawyer George

Desnoes (another past student). These loans had to be repaid, and this is where the mango crop came in.

Mom knew of a Mrs. Hall who ran a canning business out of a backyard factory in Kingston. Mrs. Hall wanted to make mango nectar and, after some experimenting with different types of mangoes, found that three varieties made an excellent blend. Bendon had ample supplies of two – black mango (actually a small sweet mango that keeps its green colour when ripe) and Number 11 (I have no idea where the name came from!). Arrangements were made in 1960 to supply Mrs. Hall with as many of these fruits as we could, and we were pressed into service. The Number 11 mango trees were huge, with wide-spreading limbs, and the protocol was that only unblemished fruit were acceptable. That translated into me or Chris climbing forty or fifty feet into the air, shinnying out another thirty feet or so on each limb in turn and shaking off the ripe fruit into a catcher (made of four bed sheets that had been sewn together) stretched out beneath the tree much like a fireman's body catcher. The old Plymouth station wagon would be driven out into the fields and cardboard boxes loaded with the fruit. Back seats removed to make space for the load and suspension locked and groaning, mom and dad would drive to Kingston and sell the fruit.

Growing up on a farm gives one a different perspective than the city dwellers. One learns that there are no free lunches and that reward and effort are closely tied. My mother never liked this one aspect on the cycle of life on the farm, and that had to do with how non-contribution was rewarded. Our cows were all given names and that personalized the anguish in her when a cow grew old and less productive, and had to be disposed of. These were not retired on the 'back 64' since there was no excess of land for that purpose. They were sold to the butcher. To her this was heartless, and went against her belief that true service should be rewarded – a somewhat liberal view, that could not survive in the circumstance. In a business with somewhat limited resources I now recount this story to underachieving staff. I have no back 64 so buck up. The butcher awaits.

Looking around at others life experiences, I see many that had more growing up, but for some strange reason the human spirit does not seem to be rewarded by having things. It is the quality of one's surroundings and early upbringing that seems to make the difference. This is best epitomized by our friend Mr. Coombs.

Byron Coombs and Spring Garden Estate

We met Byron Coombs in 1957 just after he returned from the USA. He simply showed up on our front step one day and introduced himself. He had just bought Spring Garden Estate in Bushy Park and had great plans to grow vegetables for export to the USA. He also had the vision of starting a chicken business where he would import fertile eggs, hatch them and then grow them into broilers. Little did we know that this was the start of Jamaica Broilers, the largest chicken operation in the islands.

Byron had earlier established Coombs Cold storage on Bond Street in Kingston, which imported meat from the USA and retailed directly to the public. He felt that he could grow his own chickens commercially instead of importing from the USA and dropped by to ask my dad what he thought of the idea and to invite him to visit Spring Garden to see the start-up of the operation. Dad was flattered to be asked for advice and quickly accepted. Farm life in those days often meant visiting fellow farmers to exchange ideas and generally to socialize and we had been on many trips to different parts of the island to spend a Saturday with other families on their farms.

We visited Spring Garden a week later. Byron had set up a tent and had chairs and tables set out for company. In what we later realized was typical Coombs style, there was a chef in a white hat next to what we learnt was an American-style barbecue cooker. I had never seen a real chef before and wondered at the purpose of the tall white hat. Three cars were parked off to the side, Byron's Mercedes-Benz, a Ford and a strange little bug-shaped vehicle belonging to the older Coombs son. This was the first Volkswagen beetle to be imported into Jamaica. The third car belonged to Sydney Levy, Byron's partner who would eventually buy out Byron's interest in the chicken business.

A field of odd-looking plants was in luxuriant growth to one side. We had never seen green peppers before and when invited to test that they were in fact, not at all hot, I recall wondering at the purpose of a pepper that was not hot. This was the first commercial planting of green peppers in Jamaica and Byron had already sold the crop to an American supermarket chain. He told my dad that he planned to plant more than one hundred acres by the next year and fertilize this with the droppings from the chicken houses. We had only seen small-scale vegetable operations and something that was so vast and so well-integrated was impressive. The next field over held a ripening crop of cucumbers and again I had never seen cucumbers grown on trellises but Byron explained that the American consumer was discerning and that they would not tolerate the yellow patches were the fruit to rest on the ground.

Lunch was another surprise. The chef showed us enormous t-bone steaks and asked us individually how we wanted them cooked. Byron suggested that steaks in America were usually eaten rare and that we should try it. Only my brother Chris was brave enough to order his rare and when it came, leaking blood, he dug into it declaring it great. This was the tenderest beef I had ever tasted. The beef we normally ate was from the Spanish Town market and was usually that from a worn-out dairy cow that was on its last legs or from some runt that was raised on "long pasture". Long pasture was the name used to describe the public roadsides where many of the scavenging cows belonging to landless farmers found forage. Byron declared that it was the finest prime meat from the USA. He had obviously adopted the best of American habits.

The next task at hand was to record for posterity the laying out of the foundation of Jamaica Broilers' very first chicken houses. Sydney Levy dutifully used his 8mm-movie camera to capture Chris, Steve and me stretching out the tape measure and marking the foundations of the first coop. It was well staged with a laughing Byron and my dad visible in the background.

We had been told to bring swimming trunks and after the filming Byron's son took us kids off to the old Verley Great House. The Great House was set in a small valley at the foot of the hills and by this time was in advanced disrepair. The house and pool had been built in the early 1800s but were abandoned in the late 1930s when the family lost interest in farming, cut the property into two large farms and sold these to the Perry family. Coombs had just bought the northern section from the Perrys. There was a glorious pool in the landscaped front yard and though it was fairly shallow, it had been designed with some architectural thought, with a series of pools spilling over small waterfalls from one to the other. The pool dividers all held statues of animals and mythical figures carved from soft limestone, strategically placed at the corners and waterfalls. It was obviously based on something in France. The powerful flow of water was fed directly from the spring that gave the property its name, and it was slightly milky with dissolved limestone. The bottom of the pool, no longer maintained, was covered with a layer of sand and it was teeming with fish. Colossal guango trees shaded the entire pool area, letting little warming sunlight through. Typical of spring water in Jamaica, it was a cold seventy-two degrees and we were soon shivering and glad to get out.

We were then taken down a dusty farm road to a spot where the spring widened into a large natural pool and young Coombs went to the front of his VW beetle and to our surprise emerged with three sectional fishing rods. Byron had thought of everything to influence our dad. I had never fished with a rod before and on the first throw managed to tangle the line in an impenetrable bird's nest. Fishing with hand lines after that, we caught and released (another strange American habit) at least twenty large fish.

After we returned home, dad told us that Byron wanted to attract contract farmers and had approached him to be one of the first. The arrangement was that contract farmers would finance and build their own chicken coops, probably placing them on the margins of the farm fields. The company would supply day-old chicks and all the feed needed to take them to maturity. Then, when the chickens were grown, the company would come and catch them and take them off to be processed. The farmer would be paid on the net weight of the crop, with deductions if too many chickens died. Dad seriously considered this but had to decline when he could not get financing to build the coops since he was already overextended by the mortgage on Bendon.

Byron was a great entrepreneur, one of Jamaica's greatest to my mind, and although he had to sell his interest in Jamaica Broilers he remained active, starting a number of other businesses. Seeing what he was able to do in just a few years has been something of an inspiration to me and influenced my decision to go into business many years later. He had gone off to the United States, a young black man, yet seemed to shrug off any prejudice that he encountered, picking up ideas for starting entrepreneurial enterprises in Jamaica when he returned home. This was also my first exposure to a bit of American culture and my young mind was impressed by this country where people ate raw meat, unblemished vegetables and pepper with no fire and made fishing rods that could be disassembled for transport. This must be a great country!

My dad remained a friend of Byron for many years even though he could not participate in his businesses. Jamaica Broilers went on to become a powerhouse company run by the Levy family who bought out the Coombs investment. I was to meet Byron one last time in about 1964 and even though he had aged he remained gracious and kind. I had gone to the Glass Bucket Club in Half Way Tree with my cousin Anthony just after graduating from high school and ran into Byron sitting near the dance floor surrounded by a bevy of attractive young ladies. Wise to the ways of young men, he invited us to his table and introduced us. "I am an old man and too tired to dance with all of my young nieces, Paul, will you help me?" Nieces indeed!

I must tell you that, as I write this, I am overwhelmed thinking about how hard it must have been on my parents to keep trying, to keep thinking up ways to get by while being knocked down by bad weather, crop failure, petty theft and a system that limited one's choices. The ability to pick oneself up after a setback was not so much a sign of outstanding character as it now is, it was simply what people did every day since there was no choice, no unemployment check, no social security. As a child, their struggle was never apparent to me, and we lived what seemed to be an ideal life. Every Sunday dad sat in the car smoking his pipe (a habit Bendon's cost eliminated a few years later) and reading his *Daily Gleaner* while the rest of the family was in church, after which we would go to the beach, and we always had a sit-down Sunday lunch with the requisite roast beef and Yorkshire pudding. I am sad that my parents did not survive into our better earning years when we could have rewarded their efforts, although I don't believe that they strove for material things. Mom was businesslike and relentless in seeing that everyone around her, including nieces, nephews, maids and farm workers lived up to their potential and if they rose above their circumstances, that was her reward. Yet she was tolerant and made many lifelong friends from all strata of society. Dad was consummately at ease with anyone, from a farmhand to the Governor and his easy-going confidence led him to form long-lasting friendships without the props and trappings that were so often a part of Jamaican society. In another place and time, different paths would have been open to them. Perhaps dad, a math prodigy, would have gone to high school, and completed his degree at Columbia University. That pipe might have looked better in academia. Mom would have been a relentless CEO, getting the most out of her people, much like my sister Mary now does. She sure did more with a smaller budget that any CEO I know.

Chapter four

Friendship Primary School

M y mother ran a front-porch school from about 1948–53 at our farm on Featherbed Lane. She did this primarily to earn some additional income by giving extra lessons to the Nunes children, Nigel and Melody, but also to home-school her five kindergarten-age children. I would sit in on classes as a small child, but by the time I was six I was becoming bored and disruptive and it was clear that more formal schooling was needed. I started at Friendship Primary in January 1953 in Miss Jackson's "A" class.

Friendship was a one-room Government school where the headmaster sat supreme on a platform at one end facing all eight classes, A, B and 1-6. Teacher Williams was the deranged headmaster who lived in the headmaster's cottage on the school compound with his wife and two daughters. He was a short 5'6" against Mrs. Williams who was close to six feet tall and he carried a compensating attitude. He was universally disliked because of his tyrannical ways. This did not mellow with age.

The school was a half-mile walk for me each morning and along the way I would invariably meet up with my buddies and race to the schoolyard so that we could play until the bell rang. I was the only white kid at that school. There was little traffic on St. John's road at that time and aside from the vicious mongrel dogs rushing out of the tenement yards on Featherbed Lane, the walk was a simple one, even for a six year old.

School started promptly at nine o'clock in the morning with the ringing of the school bell. That task was given over to one of the sixth class boys and he would ring the hand-held bell with a style and rhythm in keeping with his now elevated station in life. The doors were then locked and any child who came late was put to kneel around the headmaster's platform. "Rule Britannia" was then heartily sung, though few of us knew the significance of the words. Who in the heck was Britannia and how can someone rule waves? So we would turn the words around and sing "Britannia waves the rules", to our eternal amusement, though under threat of maiming if the headmaster heard. After the headmaster led the school in a prayer, "God Save the Queen" was belted out in honour of the monarch. Although we all understood she lived in a far off country, we could not figure out why she needed to be praised each morning. Now cleansed of any evil by the Psalm he had just read, the headmaster would whip out his leather strap, inappropriately named "Jacob" and methodically whip all latecomers across the back. The thick leather strap was about three inches wide and about four feet long and would reside coiled like a cobra in his back pocket when not in use. The whipping was an everyday occurrence and seldom would a child graduate without feeling the sting of Jacob. Not all children accepted the strap and every once in a while upper-class boys would be called to hold the victim while he or she was showered with blows across the back. I recall a girl bolting one morning, followed in hot pursuit by a quickly deputized posse of sixth-class boys. She was barefooted and when cornered at the barbed wire fence by St. Johns Road, she dived down a filthy drainage gutter to get away. She was unceremoniously hauled back to the school, wailing loudly and covered in mud, and put to kneel at the platform. She was then put to the strap once per hour for the rest of the school day.

Most of the students were children of the local workers and since all had pre-school duties such as fetching water from the community standpipe it was surprising that so few actually came late. A child's mind works in strange ways as I recall wishing that I too had the opportunity to walk with four gallons of water on a "cotta" on my head like these poor kids. The majority wore no shoes and probably had one set of school clothes. I quickly formed friends with many of them, never seeing any difference in status in a society that had strong class structures. In retrospect I believe that our parents wanted us all to go to a Government-run primary school instead of a private school so that we could understand that even though we were a bit more prosperous than our peers, we were in no way different. That lesson has stuck with all of us through life. We were subjected to almost all the same discipline as the other kids but none of us was ever beaten by Teacher Williams and this was probably the only pass that we were allowed. In retrospect there was an obvious double standard at play here – the poor children were subjected to corporal punishment but the children of the families with some stature in the society were spared. I think it was mostly that Teacher Williams feared the consequences of brutalising the children of people who could have him removed from his job, a universal trait of bullies. Regardless, the daily beatings were frightening to us all, even though corporal punishment was normal in a society where judges frequently sentenced offenders to the 'Cat-O-Nine' for even minor crimes. This bye was not afforded in high school, though, as the cane was applied equally to all offenders. The British were great disciplinarians and strong believers in the philosophy "spare the rod and spoil the child", so even though this may seem an anachronism in modern times, it was standard practice that ran through everyday life.

As a result of the fact that St. Johns Road had so little traffic, every time a car or truck trundled by, the entire student body would rise to peer out the schoolhouse windows. The Gilpin-Hudson family from Guanaboa Vale property had just acquired a new Mercedes Benz motor car, and if it was that car, the murmur "Look pan the Mercy-deez!" would arise from all two hundred and eighty students. The skies were even emptier in these early post-war days and the growl of a propeller-driven DC3 or even the more infrequent four-engined Super Constellation would empty the schoolroom, as everyone would rush outside to witness the rare event. The first jet passenger plane to fly into Jamaica was Pan American Airlines' Boeing 707 and I recall the first flight, sitting directly under the flight path as it thundered across the sky, leaving us all to wonder what the future held. It was loud, it was smoky and it was magnificent. It was at that moment that I knew that I too would fly some day.

There were two fifteen-minute breaks, one at 10.30 a.m. and the other at 2.30 p.m. sandwiching a one hour lunch break. My parents would expect me home for lunch each day and this bothered me since it meant that I was missing out on the marvellous treats the other children would enjoy. The headmaster would not allow any vendors on the school grounds so three or four market women would arrive and set up at the gate and display their wares in glass-fronted cases. The cases held a dazzling array of local delicacies such as Dukunu (blue drawers), pink and white-coloured grater cake, cut cake, codfish fritters and oranges. However, the orange man was my favourite. He would pull up to the school gate with his pushcart loaded with some unfortunate farmer's praedial-larcened oranges and, using a contraption with a handle that he would turn like an ice cream bucket, he would cleverly peel the orange creating a continuous thin string of rind. I think the spectacle of the orange rind unwinding always drew a curious crowd and probably added at least 1 penny to the cost of an orange, but boy was the spectacle worth it.

The morning and afternoon breaks were a flurry of activity with both sexes separating into different playgroups. The younger children would just frolic around and play catch, an adaptation of American baseball or English Rounders. The older girls would go off and play with stick dolls, jacks, start a game of hopscotch or just gossip about the boys. The older boys would set up games of gig or marbles. A gig was a home-made spinning top. These gigs were hewn from guava, calabash or lignum vitae wood into a rounded cone, then a nail would be hammered in at the point and sharpened. Sometimes the nail was three inches long. Gigs were usually hand-carved from lumps of wood and it was unusual that they were balanced – shapes differed from perfect cones to stubby egg-shapes, though the fortunate kid who had a friend with access to a wood lathe would have perfect gigs. A game of gig had two objectives. The first was winning a penny that started out buried in a hole inside a six-foot circle by being the one to move it outside the circle with his gig. The second objective was to split other gigs – they were fair game if they did not spin or if they stayed inside the circle after spinning. Their owners launched the gigs with a great deal of vigour, usually with the sharpened nail held upward between the fingers with a length of braided cord wrapped around the gig providing the spin with a quick downward slinging of the arm. The owner would line up the coin or the unfortunate opponent's gig with his bare big toe, raise the other leg like a baseball pitcher and, if the launch was accurate, the other gig would be split wide open by the sharpened point of the descending gig. The gigs would each have their own personality and song as they spun and the circle would be surrounded by a group of students who would cheer if any gig spun out in the circle. I was never any good at this despite hours spent just trying to get my gigs to spin other than on their sides or top.

Marbles were usually played with scods (small black seeds from the teak tree), horse eyes (the two-inch sized seed from a seaside plant of some sort) or marbles as the target and a large steel ball, known as an "I-anie" (Iron-i after the metal), as the weapon. The steel balls were often large ball bearings up to four inches in diameter and were said to come from train wheels. The horse eye was a flattened brown orb with a darker brown stripe along the rim. The object was to roll the I-anie and use it to dislodge the scods, marbles or horse eyes from the circle. There was one boy nicknamed Scod and I often wondered why he was given that name yet was never allowed to play. Apparently he had arrived at school one day with a pocketful of scods and only after one had been squashed by a large I-anie was it discovered that he had in fact dried out goat droppings and tried to slip them into a game as a substitute. Some boys walked with large bags of marbles as a sign of their prowess and these obvious winners would find great favour with the girls.

In the dry months around the Christmas period, the Poinciana tree in the back corner of the school compound held lots of attention. It was easy to climb and at that time of year in was in full bloom, spreading its blossoms in scarlet brilliance. But it was the pods of the unopened flowers that we sought for the game of cock-fight. Peeling off the soft covering revealed the folded stamens and these would be plucked out, with opposing fighters locking pollen-heads to see who could behead the opposition by quickly pulling on your stamen. Strategy was key, and from a distance it looked like two people breaking a wishbone.

One of my friends was John Hilton. John's father worked for the irrigation authority that ran the Rio Cobre water system and he was perhaps the only other middle class student there. It is unclear how he came to attend Friendship since he lived miles away on Monk Street in Spanish Town. Every time an airplane flew over during recess, John would relate a story about his flying machine. He claimed that his dad had made a contraption out of plywood that was mated to a bicycle, with the chain driving a propeller. To add to the story, his neighbour also had an airplane and the two of them would take off and have midair dogfights, in true Red Baron and Sopwith Camel style. I was never sure if John was telling the truth but did he ever tell a good story about soaring through the clouds.

Each year we learned to expect a few different groups to arrive and upset the school schedule. The school inspectors would arrive to check on the progress of the students although I can't recall them ever speaking to a student. The parish nurse would arrive each year just before the summer holiday and the entire student population would be vaccinated against typhoid or some other disease. In those days the same syringe would be used for each child, but the needle would be swapped out after each shot and replaced by one that had been sterilizing in a kidney-shaped vessel heated on a portable stove fuelled by purple methylated spirits. The memory is as strong as the syringe was large and all the girls would be sobbing before they got their shots. The other memory I have of visitors was when the school would receive gifts from the American government of cheese, milk powder and butter. The cheese was an orange-red, soft waxy treat that would be cut out of large cheese tins and every student would be given about a pound to take home. I thought that the USA must have been a large and generous country to afford such a wonderful gift.

The six-year-olds started in "A" class at the back of the schoolhouse and would move to "B" class at seven, working up to sixth class at age fourteen. That was the total schooling allowed to most children. In the first year, we learned the alphabet, numbers and a curious mix of manners and rules befitting the social rank of the masses. Our writing tablet was a slate with a wooden frame but many of the poor children broke theirs and sometimes ended up with just a small triangular piece to write on. I skipped "B" class and was moved to Class 1 in my second year. Here we were taught our times tables, some writing and some British history. Our writing book was called an "exercise" book and for Classes 1 and 2 it was double-lined for writing practice. These books all had the picture of a very young Queen Elizabeth on the front page that matched her picture hanging on the wall high above the headmaster's desk. I again skipped a class and moved to third and when I was ten I did the secondary school entrance exam and moved on to St. Jago High School.

I have few other memories of Friendship school, except that it seemed to have been the roosting place for thousands of canaries. It was curious since we would see few of these birds during the day, yet just before sunset the birds would descend in flocks and with loud quarrelsome chirping would perch in the dozen or so acacia trees that lined the school yard. Their arrival each evening was perhaps a sign that even in a place with such discord, beauty does appear. Teacher Williams was eventually moved from the school about five years after I left and we lost contact with him.

Chapter five

Veranda Conversations

*T*hursday evenings were set aside for Uncle Frank who would arrive from Kingston with a car full of friends, but this was not the only evening that our veranda at Featherbed Lane saw animated conversation. A constant stream of neighbouring farmers and friends would drop in unannounced, as was the habit in a country with few rural telephones. Visitors helped ease the tedium of country living in that era before television.

"Basil, I think the pilot didn't see the runway because of the rain that night and that he just fly the plane into the ground!" Wally Newman contended, waving his arms to make the point.

"But Wally, surely you don't land an airplane that way, he must be using his altimeter or something – Paul, how do they tell how high they are when they are landing?" dad handed off to me to counter Wally.

"Mr. Newman, the co-pilot reads off the height above the runway as they come in and the captain will pull back on the stick and land when the correct height is called," I offered.

"Young man, you don't know anything! Just last week I saw a movie where John Wayne landed a big bomber after all the rest of the crew was killed, and I didn't see nobody calling out any feet!" he countered. "You know about small planes, but in the big planes the pilot look out the window and when the ground is close he just lands the plane using his judgment. It was raining hard that night in Montego Bay and the glare of the lights dazzle him and he just slam the plane into the ground!" he insisted in a combination of Jamaican English and Patois (Jamaican Creole) in which tenses were mixed fluidly, feeling that he had finally won the argument. My dad would not indulge further debate, not wanting to offend a family friend and the conversation drifted to other topics.

Wally and Babs were close friends who would visit about every three weeks. Babs was the anaesthesiologist at Spanish Town Hospital and Wally was a branch manager at the Bank of London and Montreal in Kingston. They always had interesting stories that would inevitably lead to a debate. In this case it was about an Avianca Airlines flight from Bogotá to New York that had crashed in Montego Bay while landing to refuel. The route was travelled daily and it was a mystery how an experienced captain could crash a new Lockheed Super Constellation and kill half the passengers at a familiar airport in fairly good weather. The mystery was never solved as the three cockpit crew perished in the crash and back then there were no black box recording devices. Verandah experts had opinions, even those that had never so much as set foot on an airplane, and incidents like this fuelled conversations on warm summer evenings.

The Newmans were descendants of Germans who had migrated to Jamaica from Bremen in the 1830s and 1840s as agricultural workers to replace freed slaves. Most of these Germans landed at Rio Bueno and proceeded to work at sugar cane farms in St. Mary and Trelawny, but with mortality exceeding 40% in the first year because of tropical diseases and the heat, the survivors moved to Seaford Town, Ulster Spring and other towns in the cooler mountains. The distinct German population survived well into the 1980s although many of the youth moved to urban centres for better jobs. Wally retained the blue eyes and blonde hair of his ancestry and fitted well into an emerging middle class of mostly fair skinned professionals that was not tied to agriculture, Government or to the retail trade. The entrepreneurs of the immediate post-independence period were drawn mainly from this pool of educated and confident individuals and it was this group that felt most threatened by the socialist policies of the government of the 1970s. Many migrated to Canada and the USA.

The Governor's Ball

"Monica, you heard what happened at King's House last Saturday night?" Uncle Frankie always thrived on others' misfortunes and could not help himself when the British Governor and his wife were involved.

"Lady Foot had this big dinner party and since some of the guests were foreigners, she decided to go local and serve ackee & saltfish," he snickered. Ackee was considered to be poor man's food and had the dubious reputation of sometimes poisoning people.

"It seems that as a test she had the maid feed some of the ackee to her dog just to make sure that the ackee was OK. After an hour the dog was still alive so she served the ackee to her guests, obviously wanting to impress them with her local credentials. Apparently everybody ate heartily, congratulated the lady on her choice of entrée and then wandered out onto the porch to enjoy Blue Mountain coffee, cigars and cocktails. Lady Foot then asked the server how the dog was doing and got the reply: 'The dog dead, ma'am.'"

"Ambulances were called and the entire dinner party of twenty guests was rushed off to the Kingston Public Hospital to have their stomachs pumped. The next morning everyone was released and Lady Foot was able to interview the maid in more detail," Frankie recounted, bursting into laughter. "'Where is the dog?' asked Lady Foot. 'Same place where the car lick 'im, ma'am.'" He was literally rolling on the ground with laughter by the time he got to the end of this story.

" Frankie, behave yourself and stop telling lies on poor Lady Foot! She is a nice lady who you must respect because she is the Governor's wife!" chided Sybil, my mom's lifelong friend who had recently married an officer in the British regiment stationed in Jamaica. "She has enough problems dealing with the likes of Busta, who is an uncouth fellow and undeserving of being Chief Minister!" referring to Sir Alexander Bustamante, the new Chief Minister. "We had none of these social problems when the English were in charge, and here is the Governor trying to be gracious and this is the thanks he gets. We would have been much better off with Mr. Manley, who at least knows about manners!" Norman Manley had been the prior Chief Minister. "Do you know that Busta took his Buick motor car on the ship to England last year just so that he could show the Queen that he had a better car than she did?"

This was in the waning days of colonial rule and Sir Hugh Foot was sent by the British Foreign Office to work out a deal for ending colonial rule. I sat there squirming at the conversation since I knew that Dad was a firm supporter of Sir Alexander. It seemed that the city folks all liked Norman Manley for his intense intellect – he was a Rhodes Scholar and a trial lawyer who never lost a case. They wanted to somehow preserve intellectual leadership, guessing that this would be a wise path to retaining some of the pomp of colonial rule. My dad did not like the socialist tendencies of Manley and was a solid friend of Busta, who he felt, would be a better leader despite his social flaws. These pre-independence days revealed that people had very different ideas about Jamaica's future. There were those who wanted colonial rule to continue, those that supported a managed economy, those that supported federation with the other islands and those that supported an independent Jamaica. My dad supported the latter but politics were never discussed on the verandah among friends; my dad would skilfully steer the conversation in another direction.

I found it interesting that our parents would retain friendship with people with drastically different political agendas and many with deep flaws of character, many of whom, from my early teen outlook, I would have actively avoided. This was a strength on their part as it turns out, and other than a few pompous asses, my dad never met anyone that he did not like.

Mr. Clough

"David, I heard from Frankie that you just won the last two pigeon races. Tell me about it," Mom asked David Clough one evening.

"Well Monica, the trick is a simple one I picked up during the war years in London. One of my buddies was in the signal corps and was responsible for carrier pigeons. His pigeons were air-dropped to the French Resistance towards the end of the war and the Resistance would use the pigeons to send messages back to England."

"What he did was to use a plastic egg. He would open it and put a beetle in and then put that into the nest of a mother pigeon that was setting on eggs. When time came to send birds off to France, he would grab that mother pigeon knowing that the scratching of the beetle would have fooled her that the baby was about to hatch, so when the French let that bird go it would fly like hell back to the nest in London!"

David then went on to tell us how he had set up his dovecot so that returning birds would not just land on the roof where he could not get to them to clock in the time. Apparently the racing birds all had a small device attached to their leg which was needed to trigger a time-stamp machine to record their arrival time. Prior to the redesign of the pigeon roost area he had spent many a day trying to coax the returning racers down from the roof top so he could clock them in. I believe that David in his fervour to win would go as far as shooting the pigeon, if that was the only way to get them to come down off the roof.

David was a white Jamaican who thrilled at living on the dole while in London in the 1940s and would recount happy stories of how the English still had outhouses then, yet he would complain of substandard housing in Jamaica. Pigeon racing was his main interest. After discovering that he had a high leisure preference, he left the nasty business of earning a living to his wife, retiring at about age 45 to concentrate on becoming Jamaica's best pigeon racer. Though he had the humour of a cockney labourer and was the life of any party, his wife finally figured out that he should be working. They scraped together some capital and used this to start a small supermarket on Molynes Road, but that failed within two years.

David was typical of some middle class Jamaicans who liked the life that the British lived and though he did not fight the concept of the island getting independence, he would have preferred to retain the status quo and have the English dole available, if needed. But as long as his wife earned a decent living, he was okay with that, as long as she valued his leisure as much as he did.

Mr. Nairn

"And I crawl on my belly in the dark 'till I could make out their shadow in the moonlight thieving my water," Mr. Nairn recounted as he sprawled out on the front step showing us how he had sneaked up on the water thieves.

"Then I shout 'Police! Put up yu' hand!' You should see them scatter away after that, but I could recognize them even in the dark," he said with chin jutting out and a deadly serious look on his face. Most of the small farms in the area were less than two acres in size and were irrigated by the Rio Cobre irrigation works. However, because of the land settlement policy of giving every farm frontage on the main road, the farms were very deep and narrow so the irrigation feeder canals had to pass through many properties to get to Nairn's. In dry times it was not unknown for upstream farmers to illegally tap into these feeders and it became a cat and mouse game to catch them in the act since they only did the diversions at night.

Mr. Nairn was a neighbour who had saved his money while working on the Panama Canal back in 1912 and had used it to buy many small plots of land in the parish of St. Catherine, some as far as ten miles away in Bog Walk. He was a weather-beaten, rail thin man in his sixties who could be seen daily driving his donkey cart to his properties and returning home in the evenings loaded down with produce. Most of these plots had tenants, but that was just for the rent: Old Nairn was the one who cultivated the land and he would often drop by to give fruits to us. We would get navel oranges by the bagful and the odd jackfruit, but my recollection is of the exotic citron and shaddock that he would show up with every once in a while. For some reason he would decline invitations from dad to come onto the verandah and would sit on the front step. Perhaps it was some sort of social taboo he learnt growing up poor, though his net worth probably exceeded my dad's.

This conversation was typical of many that dad had with the small farmers and poor people in the area that would show up for advice when they had problems with each other or with the law. Dad was the Justice of the Peace in the area, and since he was seen as fair, they would seek him out. Invariably many of these problems would end up in Petty Session Court where the magistrate was also a JP, so it also made sense to get a feel for how a case may be handled.

We once had a cousin from California visit with her new husband and since Spanish Town had nothing attractive to tourists and sensing boredom in the couple, mom suggested that I take them to the courthouse where dad was presiding that day. The unusual thing about Petty Sessions was that judgments were not always made based on the law but on what looked equitable – an always superior method when dealing with folks who did not know how the laws worked. As a striking example of this, the case that stood out that day was one of a stolen cow. The accuser had lost a heifer a year earlier and in his testimony stated that he was walking down the road one day and saw this cow that was clearly his. When he tried to lead it away, he was accosted by the accused and a confrontation was only stopped by the intervention of a passing constable. Accusations were exchanged but there was no brand or identifying mark on the cow that could confirm ownership. The accused seemed to have a reasonable explanation for where he got the heifer and the case was a stalemate. The pleading of the accused was poignant and quite convincing and he told the court that he had a large family that depended on this cow for milk and that it would create great hardship if he lost it. In this case dad had no grounds to find on either party's behalf and made one of the strangest decisions I had ever seen. He decided that both parties owned the cow and that the accuser should take possession of it but would have to let the accused milk the cow and keep half the milk, while the accuser would keep every other calf that the cow bore in exchange for the costs of feeding the cow. Oddly, both seemed happy with the equity of the decision.

The Country Surveyor

G.K. Rose, known as Ken, was another former student of dad's at Jamaica College in the 1920s. He had gone on to become quite wealthy in his trade as a land surveyor. He had recently bought the Handal property next door to ours on Featherbed Lane and would come over on some weekends to be sociable. He was very much the gentleman farmer who grew no crops but kept the farm in part as a stable for his valuable racehorses. Almost every weekend he would arrive with his friends to play cards and drink expensive Scotch Whiskey and we were accustomed to seeing many of the wealthy of Jamaica in tow for the weekend. One fixture was Charlie Babcock, a Canadian who was a radio announcer with the handle 'The cool fool with the live jive'.

The country surveyor of mid-century Jamaica was constantly busy and not above taking a bribe of a few pounds to move a property line. Ken Rose told a story one day of one of his colleagues who, many years earlier, had 'adjusted' a boundary to place a large mango tree on his client's property in exchange for ten pounds sterling. There was some initial grumbling by the neighbouring farmer who lost the tree but he finally accepted the survey on the basis that a brown man would probably know better than he did, and at any rate how could he challenge a decision as a poor illiterate man.

Time went by, and with memory dimmed the same surveyor was called to survey the neighbour's property; forgetting that he had earlier adjusted the line, he snickered about the idiot that must have made the mistake and promptly fixed the problem. The tree was returned to the rightful owner.

He was then accosted by the other landowner. "I paid you ten pounds to give me that tree fifteen years ago and now you take it away!"

"You've had that tree damn long enough so stop complaining!" was his response.

This incident typifies a problem that started to emerge throughout the country with merchant, land developer and other educated classes using guile to dispossess those of little means. It was not yet that common a problem, to be sure, but when it happened it was a social crime that was seldom punished. We saw this from time to time and it would always grate on dad's nerves, forcing him to take it up as a cause. After the devastation of Hurricane Charlie in 1951, there were gangs of Parish Councillors, elected officials, who would resell donated goods to the poor. The medium-sized farmer class in Jamaica was a stabilizing force in those days, acting as a sounding board for emerging disputes and acting in an unofficial capacity between the labouring classes and the government to tamp down issues that could easily become problems. These farmers also supplied needed employment in areas where there were few alternatives and the mass exodus of farmers, fearing that their land would be taken by the Government in the 1970s, removed this stabilizing influence and opened the country to more lawlessness than might otherwise have occurred. In later years, corruption crept into the police force and the customs officials as never before, interfering with the rule of law. It is not now uncommon to be stopped by the traffic police and to hear "What you have for the officer?"

The Palestinians

"Zionists are going to be the death of the Palestinians and if we don't mind sharp, start a third World War!" shouted Johnny Handal in surprisingly good English. My mother squirmed in her seat, her part-Jewish ancestry and her many Jewish friends and relatives causing her to feel conflicted about Palestine. How could she reconcile the Handal's situation of being forced off their land in Palestine in 1948 with the fate of a Jewish people who had endured so much repression throughout history?

The Handals had been allowed to migrate to Jamaica from a camp in Lebanon only because they had influential relatives in Jamaica. They quickly raised capital from their network of family and friends and put their agricultural skills to work on the farm next door, where they grew rice and sugar cane. Johnny had a university degree in agriculture from Jordan, was a driven person who pined for his lost existence in the Palestine and held deeply felt and enduring resentment. The Handals had been Christians in a land of mostly Moslems, and migrated and lived as a family group of mother, two brothers and their wives, and two sisters at the family farm. Mother Handal wore a black burqa, Moslem dress, as everyday dress which was strange to us given her Christian religion. Victor, the older brother, married a beautiful Haitian lady named Victoria, who initially spoke no English but found solace with my grandmother, who was also Haitian, until she picked up some English.

It was through this family that we were introduced to the dishes of the Levant, as there was a constant flow of food across Featherbed Lane. Dad liked labneh, a type of yoghurt. We all feasted on kibbeh, muttabel, hummus and baklava. These dishes have now found their way into mainstream Jamaica, much like Indian and Chinese dishes that are so much a part of everyday life.

The people from the Levant saw very few of their numbers leave the shores of Jamaica during the difficult 1970s. They had already left a beloved, though dysfunctional, homeland once and were perfectly capable of working around whatever regulations any Government could impose. After intifadas, holocausts and crusades, countless invasions and constant civil wars in their native land, Jamaica was a paradise. They are now one of the most prosperous and industrious groups in Jamaica.

The Jamaican Jews had been similarly forced from their native lands in Iberia in the sixteenth century during the Portuguese Inquisition and were some of the island's oldest families. They were established in business and oddly, the troubles in the Levant did not seem to affect the relationships between them and the more recent migrants from Syria – the name given to the areas around Mount Lebanon from whence they came.

Jamaica was a melting pot of immigrants from many countries and as it is a small place, all of these groups came in constant contact with each other. The hurt of dispossession was muted in this environment and the Handal family soon fitted in and married into other Jamaican families.

Chapter six

Summer of 1956

1 956 was a year of maturity for me and my cousins. Grandma Virtue passed away early in the year, my cousin Steve, Chris and I were each given brand new Okapi penknives, and we spent a week at the beach.

The excitement of the trip to Runaway Bay had Steve and me up before day 'a mawnin', hanging out until our parents were ready to leave. We wandered about in the front yard for a while, cleaning the thin layer of rust from our Okapis, aimlessly whittling pieces of wood and looking for some action. As we wandered out to the front gate in the half light of early morning, an old man came jiggling down Featherbed Lane on the back of a tiny donkey. His feet almost reached the ground, and it was obvious from the rapid gait of the beast that the rider and his twin-basket hampers were too heavy. The rider was humming as he rode towards us, perhaps contemplating a hard day in the cane fields – cane cutters often started before sunrise to escape the heat of the day. Instantly recognizing that this was some potential action coming down the road, we set up an ambush, hoping to scare the nuts off this person. As he reached the gate, we leapt out of the tall Seymour grass with knives brandished, expecting that we would get perhaps a yelp of surprise followed by a belly laugh once he recognized that we were 'Busha pickney dem', but we underestimated his mood. He reached for his bill (a short, stubby cutlass made for cutting cane), and looking menacingly towards us, said "What the rass you want?" It was then that I knew that Steve was destined for the bar. He broke the awkward silence with his squeaky, nervous pre-teen voice; "Hi, We just wanted to say good morning!" Our victim rode off grumbling while we lapped our tails and sprinted for the safety of the house.

As soon as the old car was loaded up, we set off for the beach. The Ford ate up the miles as we headed through a cool and foggy Bog Walk Gorge, past the hydropower station that had been built to run the electric trams in Kingston in the late 1800s, and past the huge iron pipe that channelled the river from the dam to the turbines. As we ambled along the lush breadfruit and jackfruit-lined road through Unity Village, dad recounted for the hundredth time how thirty men had drowned in that pipe some fifty years earlier. The water had been turned off so that they could clean debris from the penstock but someone had turned the water on before they were finished, trapping them. We soon entered the deepest part of the gorge, with thousand-foot sheer walls where the dam stood. Here the railway tracks emerged from the rock after a one-mile tunnel through the wall of the gorge, and road, rail and river met at the Bog Walk gantry bridge. Off to the right, the road branched over to Sligoville, the bad-weather route when the river flooded the gorge road. Off to the left we headed, through the whistle stop town of Bog Walk, past the Bybrook sugar factory and fertile fields of citrus, cane and bananas.

The Lindo family owned much of this land. Old man Harold Lindo lived on the crest of Sligoville at 2,500 feet above the valley, and for years we could see his spotlight at night from our home on the plain below – his son Harold Jr. had been an RAF squadron leader in the war and had died young, perhaps leading to the old man's quaint behaviour. We believed that in the old man's madness, triggered by the awful loss, the light was a beacon meant to lead his dead son home from his last mission over Germany.

After about three hours we arrived at the Silver Bullet, a three-bedroom cottage on a slight sea cliff above the beach at Runaway Bay. The cottage was cosy, with enough room for the entire group, and this was to be home for the next week. The beach was a wide stretch of white coral sand effectively secluded by low cliffs at each end. Fishermen shared the beach, pushing their colourful dugout canoes onto coconut trunk rollers each day after returning from the sea. Elegantly bent coconut trees shaded the beach, and there was a pleasant smell of seaweed in the shady alcove below the cliff. Other cottages shared the beach path, which split as it descended to the beach with a branch leading into a giant cleft in the cliff, emerging into a delightful rock pool full of colourful tropical fish. Here we would peer through goggles at the fish, crabs and even the odd anemone. Offshore, the breakers roared on the reef, which was separated from the beach by a sea grass-covered sandy bottom.

It was here that I taught myself to swim. As dad sat on the beach, unlit pipe hanging from the corner of his mouth, occasionally peering over his glasses at us, we would frolic in the shallow water, feeling the bottom with our toes for clams. Areas of sandy bottom would separate the patches of grass from each other and since the water was always just a few feet deeper in the sandy areas, I would push off and glide across the bare areas. Soon I noticed that the more I relaxed, the further I glided, and soon I noticed that I could propel myself by thrashing my arms.

The beach sand was all broken coral, and it was littered with the shells of various molluscs. Jamaica has almost no tide and the beach was steep and clean up to the vegetation, beyond which was a thick canopy of Jamaican Tall coconut trees with a deep layer of fallen boughs, covered by Beach Morning Glory vines. The cliff had been undercut by the pounding surf of an earlier era, and everywhere the sand was riddled by crab holes. I still remember the flop and hiss of the small breaking waves, especially at dawn when the water was at its gentlest and apparently at its warmest – the water was always warmer than the air at that time of day.

Uncle Frankie, my mom's youngest brother, arrived late in the week with the full intent of catching fish. His first target was the small colourful fish that lived in the pools at the cleft in the cliff and we spent the morning helping him corral these into glass jars. Frankie owned a tropical fish shop and this was one way to keep it stocked. The fish were generally less than two inches long and were remarkably colourful, flashing the very rainbow.

Frankie went fishing with a cane rod every night from the cliff to the east of the cottage and came back in the morning with nothing to show. We were not allowed to go with him – "Too young", according to mom.

Uncle Cliff motored in by boat from Priory Harbour, about five miles east, one morning with his good friend and fishing companion Sam Christie. Sam fished for a living and the next day we were to see this in action. First, though, we went trolling on the outside of the reef. It was my first time in a boat, and the colours of the sea, the smell of the seaweed, the roll of the swell were all wonderful. Dad and Uncle Cliff held rods, but although we fished all morning, running up and down the coast, they caught nothing. Dad had a strike on his rod, which had a spoon bait on it, and declared that it was a kingfish. We were proud that our hero could discern the specific species of fish from a quick bite deep in the ocean. We did see hundreds of flying fish taking flight with barracuda in pursuit, and at one point we passed about a dozen brightly coloured baitfish that had been cut cleanly in half by something large.

We then motored along the coast to the beach at Llandovery Falls, which was not accessible by road, and were allowed to go ashore and play in the area where the whitish-green river water plunged directly over the falls into the sand-bottomed surf. This spot was remote, devoid of humanity, and it was spectacularly beautiful.

Late that afternoon Sam took us to check his turtle traps to see if he had caught anything. These traps consisted of wood floats that were carved and painted to look like Green Turtles, which were connected to nets. The nets were stretched across the gap in the reef at Llandovery

River. Apparently this was a nesting beach for turtles and the decoys were intended to create curiosity, luring them into the nets. There were no catches, to our disappointment and this was probably because the decoys did not look enough like turtles to fool us, much less a turtle. Sam then invited us to come to Priory Bay the next morning. We would watch the villagers pull a seine net from shore and then we would go deep-sea fishing with one of his sons.

Setting the net, which was about five hundred yards long, was a morning-long exercise. The net was loaded into two open canoes that were then rowed to the inside of the reef, about a quarter-mile offshore. Priory Harbour was deep and the quarry was Goggle-eye jack. These pound-sized fish formed gigantic schools at spawning time and would gather in this spot just a few times a year. The spotters would row out and use water glasses (wooden boxes with a glass bottom) to locate the school. The word would be given and the canoes would play out the net, each heading outward in a semicircle, eventually ending with both ends taken to shore. Lead weights would take the base of the net all the way down to the sea floor, about one hundred feet, while cork floaters would keep the top on the surface. The whole village turned out and ropes at the end of the net were rhythmically hauled in to the beat of a drum. It took a full hour to retrieve the net, and as it came close to shore the excitement grew. Soon the shallows were churned to froth by the thousands of fish caught in the seine net. Dip nets were used to scoop the fish into empty canoes on the beach. This was the ultimate excitement for us kids. Not only were there multitudes of silvery goggle-eyes, but also a few snappers, barracudas and others. The sale of the fish started at once, and in a few minutes, basket-bearing ladies were carrying full loads to market.

As promised, Sam's son Malo who was home on leave from his seaman job on a bauxite ship took us fishing offshore. We travelled about ten miles offshore in search of dolphin fish and soon found a weed line of floating Sargasso. This was apparently where dolphin fish schooled and on this occasion they were there by the dozens, cruising about in electric colours. These flashy green and yellow fish would not bite that morning.

The water was inky purple and looked sinister with the midday sun's rays piercing the surface and converging as they plunged into the bottomless deep. After multiple passes through the school, Malo stopped the boat by the floating seaweed and to our amazement, donned flippers and goggles and dove overboard with a spear gun. He quickly shot a seven-pounder and tied it off to the boat, grabbed another gun and shot three more. He later told us that if you take the first fish into the boat, the school disappears, so the trick is to keep the first one caught in the water so that it remains visible to its companions. What really made an impression on us was the bravery of this man who thought nothing of diving into water that was thousands of feet deep. All manner of shark were probably down there. He was our hero.

The fishing continued, as might be expected with Uncle Cliff living close by. The very next day he picked us up on the beach in his boat and we headed back through the opening in the reef, this time turning west. About ten miles later we passed Discovery Bay and turned into Rio Bueno harbour, where Columbus landed in 1494 to fill his water casks. About a quarter mile up the river, we left the main stream and beached the boat a few yards up a tributary. The water flowed clear and fresh in the little tributary and later, as we explored, we discovered that it rose in a large blue hole only a few hundred yards upstream. The riverbank was quite a bit higher than the surrounding marshes, was draped with sensuously leaning coconut palms and was covered with crab holes. Uncle Cliff and Sam set about the serious business of catching Calipeva mullet, which was quite different from any fishing that I had ever seen. This was similar to trout fishing, so instead of some sort of meat-type bait, Sam used a dip net with a fine mesh to scoop up little clots of moss that drifted downriver and put them in a bucket. Using a very thin cane rod, with fishing line that was scarcely thicker than thread and a hook that seemed almost invisible, Uncle Cliff set about clumping the almost liquid moss around the hook and then wrapping it with a short length of thread. He would then gently direct the hook into the stream, letting it drift on the current into the turbid confluence of the two rivers where the larger fish were lurking. The bait only lasted one or two trips into the stream before it washed off and had to be replaced and I was fascinated by the patience that this method demanded. For myself, I was content to use shrimp bait and caught a half dozen pound-sized shad in the main river that morning.

Uncle Cliff only caught one fish that day but was it exciting! A six-pound mullet took the bait after countless tries and just took off down the Bengal River. The line was only four-pound test, so to slow the fish; he had to rely on skill, not brute force. Sam quickly started the motor as Uncle Cliff jumped on board so that they could chase the fish downstream. It took nearly thirty minutes for them to land this fish and the fight took them all the way into the bay. We sat on the bank marvelling at their patience and the artistry of the fight. Victor and conquered arrived back to the accolades of the spectators sitting on the bank of the Bengal and, having caught his quota of one fish, Uncle Cliff loaded us back into the boat and headed back home to Runaway Bay.

The Bengal was a fishing club that had very strict rules about overfishing and, since the little river ran entirely through the property owned by one of the members, a Mr. Hopwood, it was possible to enforce this. Two decades later, this was to come to a tragic end when a group used dynamite to kill the entire stock of Calipeva in the river. I firmly believe this was caused by food shortages and lawlessness brought on by the socialist government of the 1970s.

The holiday was over too soon and the next day we hauled our blistered, sunburnt bodies into the Ford and made our weary way home. I dreamt of this vacation for many years and was determined to learn to spearfish when I grew up. Our parents were unable to afford vacations like this very often; in fact I only recall two in my childhood, so this was very special to us all.

Chapter seven

The Fishing Trip

V ery few things rate higher on the scale of child cruelty than announcing a fishing trip with Uncle Cliff a full four months ahead of time. This announcement was to lead to the longest 122 days in my life and after the waiting, to one of my greatest adventures. Uncle Cliff wanted us to come down to Sunnyville for a week of fishing on Bucknor Banks!

Uncle Cliff, my father's younger brother, was a Presbyterian minister who was one of the most irreverent reverends that I had ever known. He had a complete disregard for anything that got in the way of his ministry to the poor; he had an easygoing charm combined with a sparkling personality that showed itself in his being one of the finest raconteurs in the island (as well as an impish tendency to call every woman a virgin). He also disregarded anything that interfered with his first love, fishing, through which he made friends from every strata of the society.

These traits were to lead to many interesting life experiences during the 1930s when he was first trying to find his place in a class-divided Jamaica. The class structures in Jamaica at that time were strict; the

British Government officers and leading planters and merchants occupied the top strata, followed by individuals in the professions; then mixed race individuals in the trades and small farmers and finally the masses of the labour force. The laws were meant to protect the upper classes, with a curious mix in the police force of English officers and black Jamaican constables asked to apply the laws.

As Jamaica had no large game animals, I often wondered why dad had needed a rifle. Perhaps it was for target shooting since he was a marksman and coach of the Jamaica College rifle team. When he quit teaching in 1929 and headed off to New York to put himself through College, Uncle Cliff inherited his Lee-Enfield .303 rifle. The rifle was unregistered, as was often the case in those days. If you have a hammer everything looks like a nail – in Uncle Cliff's mind, if you have a rifle, everything looks like a fish.

The mangroves of Jamaica's estuaries swarmed with large fish – so why not shoot them? When he had the time, Cliff would sling his rifle over his shoulder and stealthily climb into the mangroves. Looking straight down, he could see fairly deep into the clear water, and would patiently sit there until a large fish swam by. Allowing for deflection, he would dispatch it with a single shot, and then his helper would dive into the water and retrieve the fish. He grew bolder and bolder in these escapades, and lacking respect for colonial authority, soon he no longer sought to restrain his activities.

One morning he found himself on the Martha Brae Bridge shooting fish. The Martha Brae is a largish river about a mile east on the main North Coast road from the town of Falmouth. It was illegal to possess a firearm without a license; it was illegal to discharge a firearm within one hundred yards of a road and it was illegal to fish from the bridge. There were probably some other illegals in there somewhere, but to Uncle Cliff, they were all mere inconveniences. As he told the story many years later, he was on about the third Snook (a twenty-pounder) when an Austin 7 motor car clattered across the bridge then stopped about fifty yards down the road. Out came a leg and the turned head of an Englishman, who then seemed to think better of it as the door slammed and the car continued into Falmouth. About twenty minutes later, a large Jamaican sergeant of police came puffing down the road from Falmouth, riding a bicycle and sweating profusely. He was too large for the bicycle, with a large protruding belly almost on the handlebar and just the heels of his boots on the pedals, feet turned outward, cranking away in obvious discomfort. He dropped the bicycle to the ground by the side of the bridge, hitched up his pants, and walked over to Cliff, who was at this time tracking a fish as the school exited from the shadow of the bridge. As the sergeant was about to place his hand in apprehending fashion on Cliff, he backed off in curiosity. With the huge bang of a .303, Cliff took out a large Snook, and one of his assistants dived into the river to recover the spoils.

By this time the sarge was no longer curious but intrigued. The fifth fish was enthusiastically pointed out by the sarge; "See anodda one dere sir!"

As it is, .303 clips only hold five rounds and Cliff stepped back, "Oh-oh, out of ammunition!"

The sarge responded "Hold on sir, 'a soon come!" and leaping on his bike, headed into Falmouth, pedaling furiously.

Returning twenty minutes later, he strode up to Cliff and handed him a new clip of five rounds. Accepting the gift without question, but perhaps with bemused mirth, Cliff completed his fishing expedition with five more fish. Being a kindly fisherman, Cliff then said "Thank you sergeant, can I offer you a fish? How can I help you?"

The sarge responded with a little Anancy and with a diplomacy shaped by surviving for years in a bent social structure. "No thanks sir, but a de superintendent [of police] sen' me fi lock you up. But 'im a white man an' you a white man, so wha mek 'im mus' sen me? Go 'bout you business 'fore 'im come back!". Obviously touched by this diamond in the rough, Cliff formed a lifelong friendship with the sergeant, and would often stop at the Falmouth Police Station on his way to Sunnyville, the old family home in Hanover, to exchange greetings. Friendship can always overcome class and race when there is a common foe.

Cliff had befriended many in his life through fishing, including his lifelong friend, Sam Christie from Priory in St. Ann. Sam was a fisherman by trade and a large jovial man who enjoyed Cliff's company. They shared a repartee that was uncommon in those times and would often camp out along the shore, setting up a fishing camp where they would cook breadfruit and fish and sleep under the stars. They were the unofficial fishing guides to the tourist industry in its very early days before there were full time tourist fishing guides and the manager at Tower Isle Hotel would call on Cliff and Sam to take out important guests that wanted to fish. One memorable story Cliff told was about the time he was asked to take out the son of an important guest, Donald Danforth, who was the CEO of The Ralston Purina Company and son of William H. Danforth, the founder. The boy, John Danforth (later three-term Senator for Missouri), was just 15 years old at the time and managed to hook a large tiger shark. When Sam leaned over to cut the line and release the useless shark, Danforth demanded that he keep the fish and take it to show his dad at the hotel. Not having a truck to take the shark the twenty miles from Priory to Tower Isle, Cliff and Sam were forced to drape the shark lengthwise over the car roof. As soon as his dad had a chance to look at and photograph the shark, he dismissed Cliff, who was then forced to dispose of the carcass.

I clearly recall the sleepless night before the long-awaited fishing trip. I awoke before dawn and idled away the time with Steve before we all set off from Spanish Town in the family car, a 1950's kingfisher blue Pontiac station wagon, on the six-hour drive. We made the usual stops in Ewarton to fill the radiator for the climb over Mt. Diablo and at Mt. Rosser to buy tangerines, june plums, sweetsops, otaheiti apples and star apples. The drive from Moneague to Chalky Hill was a dusty twelve miles down a white-marl road laid on top of red bauxite dirt, and a plume of thick dust rose as we rumbled past the stone-stacked walls that marched across the pleasantly rolling hills of central St. Ann.

This part of the journey was through pretty countryside with a jumble of conical hills, and grass neatly cropped by cattle. The hilltops each wore a crown of trees and the occasional valley floor held a muddy cattle pond. Stone walls were everywhere, made from loose-stacked fieldstones gathered in an earlier century. They rose about four feet high and were neatly dry-stacked with no visible concrete or binding material. Besides lining the road, they climbed over hill and dale as pasture boundaries. Covered in blue Morning Glory and the vivid yellow flower of the deadly Nightshade, the stone walls were a signature feature of this parish.

We soon drove past Annandale Plantation, the ancestral home of Aunt Mabel, Uncle Cliff's wife. The entrance was set back from the road and bounded by large stone pillars. A huge silk cotton tree added some mystery to the scene as it towered over the gate and the Royal Palm trees guarding it, enveloping them with its huge buttresses and gracefully lowered branches. Jamaican folklore is filled with tales of duppies (ghosts) hanging around these huge monarchs of the forest, and as kids we believed all these stories. The driveway curved out of sight behind a hill and the great house was discretely hidden from view in the way of the very rich. Sir Thomas Roxburgh was the patriarch of the family and for years was rumoured to be a son of England's King Edward VII. Annandale and an adjacent family property covered 3,000 acres and were, like so many in this parish, cattle and pimento properties.

Thickets Estate, on the opposite side of the road, was a deliciously attractive property. The estate house was more modest than Annandale, but with a setting that was almost sensuous. Sitting on a small hill across from a small pond, this English country-style house had a beautifully manicured lawn and a Kentucky-style, triple-railed, horse fence. The attractiveness of the place is hard to describe. The slopes were just right, the house exactly in scale and in exactly the right place. Another mile up the road was the old cut-stone Presbyterian Church at Davis Town, set in a broad valley reminiscent of a Welsh country setting. This was the church where Uncle Cliff preached and was later buried. Opposite, the road branched to Arthur's Seat, the stunning property belonging to the Melville family. It sat on a hill high above Ocho Rios and had the most spectacular views. The road wound on and soon plunged around a corner, revealing the Caribbean Sea in all its cobalt glory, under a brilliant blue sky, set against the emerald green of the pimento trees that covered Roaring River property common. "I see the sea and the sea sees me, God bless the sea and the sea bless me!" we children would sing out at the first sight of the sea.

A quick left turn down a shaded lane guarded by pink, flowering Quick Stick trees led to the manse. Stopping briefly, we were greeted by the always smiling Aunt Mabel. Aunt Mabel had an eerie resemblance to Queen Elizabeth II, reinforcing the rumours of her grandfather's heritage. The manse was an old cut-stone building set on the crest of Chalky Hill, with a wide north-facing verandah where all entertaining took place. Maidenhair and other ferns covered the hillsides and even grew in the gaps between the stones of the house. The curry smell of a grass that grew in the area pervaded the place. Uncle Cliff soon joined us, and with his impish smile, joyously greeted all the 'virgins'. Everyone was a virgin to Cliff, even my mother. Having just reached the age where we knew what a virgin was, it left us in giggles. This naughty, naughty man was such a charmer! It was interesting to see how my dad would warm to his younger brother. Uncle Cliff lifted the spirits of everyone with whom he came in contact. We kids were plied with sorrel and bun and were entertained by the domestic staff until it was time to go.

Setting off down the steep, unpaved road to Steer Town, we passed the riverhead of the Roaring River and were soon on the coast at Drax Hall. The Roaring River is only about a mile long in its thousand-foot fall to the beach. It was long ago spoilt when it was coaxed from its waterfall-filled journey into a barrel-stave pipe and used to feed a hydroelectric plant. Below the plant at Laughing Waters it exits in a final, spectacular plunge into the sea.

St. Ann's Bay was the next town, and it flowed down the steep slope to a cute little harbour where Columbus lost his flagship, the

Santa Maria, on his third voyage. This town was a curious mixture of quaint well kept little houses on the hillside; a set of stately colonial Government buildings and a bustling, noisy market. On the western side of St. Ann's Bay sat the ruin of Seville, the early sixteenth century Spanish settlement. Next was the sleepy fishing village named Priory, where Uncle Cliff stopped and picked up Sam Christie. Sam loaded the outboard motor into Cliff's car and the convoy of two cars set out for Sunnyville.

I entertained my cousins Dawne and Steve by recalling the name of every village and hamlet as the Pontiac ate up great gobs of distance at the stately speed of thirty miles per hour. My mom felt that thirty was pushing the envelope on safety and dad dared not argue. Laughlands, Salem, Runaway Bay, Rio Bueno, Duncans, Falmouth all sped by. We passed through Montego Bay and Steve burst into song with "Red Sails in the Sunset" as we rounded the big curve at the airport, revealing the entire Montego Bay Yacht Club fleet silhouetted against the setting sun. At the old Great River Bridge, dad recalled how he had lost his gun in the sea in 1935. That was the year he had returned home after six years in New York with a new revolver in his suitcase. Apparently the suitcase had been strapped to the broad fender of Uncle Will's car, and both the fender and the suitcase were launched into the sea when Uncle Will collided with another car. How many cars could there have been on that stretch of road in 1935?

As it was getting dark, we drove past Round Hill Hotel and wondered which famous guest might be there now – Mr. Churchill or Princess Grace or perhaps Senator Kennedy? After passing through Hopewell, we could just make out, in the fading light of dusk, the ribs and boiler of a wrecked ship imbedded in the sand, almost on the beach. It had been there since 1922, my dad said, probably a coastal schooner that had got lost in a storm. That wreck still sits in the sand today, sloshed by each passing wave. Finally we passed Tryall, Sandy Bay and Mosquito Cove then started the climb to Jericho, arriving to a lamp-lit Sunnyville. It was sad not having Mistress greet us with her infectious laughter, yet I felt this strange fear that her ghost might appear at any time. Why this was a fear and not a joy, I have never figured out.

After an agonizingly slow day, the next evening we set off to the boat shed at Mosquito Cove. Sam carted out the 40-horse power Johnson outboard and sat it on the transom of the dugout. The boat had been hewn from the trunk of an enormous silk cotton tree; it was fully thirty feet long with a beam of seven feet and quite capable of taking our party of seven. We all loaded up and Sam pushed off from the mangrove shallows. The outboard stuttered to life in a cloud of bluish smoke, the forward gear was engaged with an audible clunk, and we slowly spluttered out into the cove.

Mosquito Cove was vaguely pear shaped, about half a mile long and rather narrower at the entrance to the sea than inland. The first few hundred yards were murky, but dead calm, perhaps because of the load of fresh water from New Works River. The next few hundred yards, after we passed the ribs of the old schooner dock, the water deepened and cleared and we could feel the beginnings of the ocean swell. Sam drove the boat slowly, close to the mangroves while Uncle Cliff positioned himself in the bow, with dip-net in hand. Every once in a while he would plunge the net into the water, and each time there would be a froth of activity as the school of mullets would explode in flight. Some would even leap into the boat, as a smiling and whistling Cliff dumped his catch, flapping, into the bottom of the boat. This was to be our bait. We were very excited, as we had only ever seen these types of fish red-eyed and dead in the bottom of the fish vendor's basket on Featherbed Lane. Here they glistened, silvery and flapping about. Unlike river fish, the life span of sea fish out of water seemed to be less than a minute, and Sam set about filleting these for the hook.

By the time we passed through the entrance to the cove, the sea was a deep-blue and the swell had picked up. The waves crashed into the headlands around the entrance and the wind freshened slightly. There were no lighthouses to mark the entrance, so we had to leave before it was dark and return the next morning in daylight. I wondered if my stomach would be able to keep up with my enthusiasm for ocean fishing. I strongly doubted it.

The sea got deep very quickly here and soon Uncle Cliff was dipping up flying fish instead of mullets, marking the change from fresh to salt water. It was a marvel to see the flying fish take to the air, gliding on their oversized fins. Sometimes when pursued by barracuda, dolphin or kingfish, they would barely touch down before taking off again, covering hundreds of yards in flight. Every dip brought in a baitfish, and after a while he would catch ballyhoo, a curious little fish with an elongated top bill that resembled a miniature marlin. Flying fish and ballyhoo seemed to be at an unfortunate point on the ocean food chain – the middle. They were the perfect metaphor for my family in Jamaican society.

The sun was starting to sink below the western horizon and the Tilley lamp was brought out, primed and lit. The fitting of a small crocheted bag over the fuel jet preceded lighting the Tilley. The pressure was pumped up on the kerosene chamber and a match touched off the flame. Soon the glass was fitted and a brilliant light eked out a circle of visibility around us. From its position out over the bow, it shone into the sea which, in addition to giving us a working light, attracted fish. Within a few minutes of lighting the lamp, a large garfish jumped into the boat and bit Chris on his heel – dangerous waters!

After a journey of about three miles, and using a sort of triangulation of lights from Montego Bay and Lucea, Sam pronounced us in a good spot – over the shallow banks. Bucknor Banks was one of a series of inshore elevations in the seafloor off the north coast of Jamaica. The water depth was generally about a hundred fathoms between the Banks and the shoreline, and further offshore the water quickly deepened to more than a thousand fathoms. On the Banks, the water depth was about fifteen to twenty fathoms. Coral and sand covered the underwater surface of the bank and it was the home for all sorts of bottom- and surface-feeding fish.

Sam dropped a plumb line, weighted by lead, and as he retrieved the line, counted the number of fathoms, measuring the line using his wingspan – they say one's wingspan is the same as one's height. He counted twenty fathoms (120 feet) – a good depth for most of the fish we were seeking – and threw out the kellet. I don't know where the term kellet came from, but it was a dead-weight anchor made from odd car parts. In our case, it was the fifty-pound crankshaft from a truck engine that we took turns pulling from the sea floor each time we changed position to find new fish.

Baiting our hooks with scraps of fish, we soon had our lines in the water. Rods were never used for bottom fishing. We used sixty-pound test line with wire leaders, unwinding line from special wooden spools until the bottom was found. On each retrieve to remove fish or replace bait taken by fish, the line would be dropped into the boat bottom in foot-wide circles, and this was kept remarkably tangle-free unless someone dropped a thrashing fish into the line! Chin on the boat gunwale, I peered into the depths, following the converging beams of the lamp until they dissipated in a swarm of plankton. The water was filled with streaks of light from the photo-luminescent plankton whenever fast-swimming fish disturbed them.

Fishing was a funny game, and this night was to be no different – two people sitting side by side, using identical lines, hooks and bait could have completely different luck. I caught fish on nearly every drop of the line while Steve had almost no bites. The next night things were to switch. The first fish we caught was a yellow tail snapper of about two pounds, and through the night we would bring in moonshine snapper – a pink-red snapper with huge eyes – then a bunch of snit, an evil-looking sort of gar with spectacularly large teeth. We caught red snapper, grunt, and a whole array of colourfully striped, speckled and polka-dotted fish. Sam rigged up a floating line baited with a whole ballyhoo and during the night caught three large kingfish. While the floating lines were out, he rigged a bamboo pole to catch goggle-eye jacks. The bait was a piece of aluminium foil at the end of about twenty feet of very light line which attracted plankton as it reflected the light from the lamp. He used just the angle of the rod to toss and retrieve the line, and when the goggle-eyes swarmed the boat in pursuit of the light-attracted plankton, he would catch a fish with almost every cast. Sam must have caught one hundred of these tasty, pound-size fish that first night. He was having great fun and he and Uncle Cliff were constantly teasing the other about who was the better fisherman. It was great camaraderie and a special bond obviously existed between these two men of such different backgrounds. Cliff reminded Sam about the time they took out one of the DeLisser men, who was blind but an ardent fisherman. He told how this man, whose family owned most of the coastal land stretching from Montego Bay to Negril, would hold up every goggle eye he caught and say "It shiny ee!" to the great amusement of all.

I was the only one to become seasick, much to the amusement of those catching fewer fish. Up until midnight I was fine. Well, not really fine, but hanging on to my lunch through sheer tenacity. The night wind caused it. In Jamaica, the north east trade wind blows obliquely along the shore all day where it is lifted by the mountains to form clouds. As the heat engine of the sun cut out there was a period of calm and at about midnight the wind reversed and flowed down from the mountains and out to sea. The night wind then comes from the land, at a right angle to the swells which did not die down with the coming of night. The swells were not all that high – maybe six or seven feet, but the bank was just shallow enough to interact with the ever-present ground swell creating steep bunched up waves. The boat then arrowed into the wind, and then took the swell from an angle, making for a twisting, up and down ride. Those who have never been seasick don't know the misery. It was a long night, as I alternated between baiting the waters and lying in the bilge asking the Lord to take me.

By sunrise the waves and the land breeze calmed down and it was time to troll. Two bamboo outriggers were tied across the seats and two rods were used as shorter outriggers. I well recall the scene that morning as the sun rose. The sea was slightly heaving from a steady, though almost imperceptible ground swell, while the surface had an almost oily appearance, with dimples from a wayward zephyr of a wind. The sea birds, especially the man-o-war albatrosses, were out skimming the waters and when we spotted them circling, that usually meant baitfish; if there were baitfish present, we could expect big fish. Weed lines, consisting of narrow lines of Sargasso weeds, were a perfect place for fish and we could troll down these lines in search of dolphin fish.

This was one of the most disappointing mornings of fishing. Steve caught a Spanish mackerel and that was it. There were large schools of tuna breaking the surface everywhere, and we circled around the area and drew the lines through the feeding frenzy, but there were no strikes. Sam speculated that there must have been so much bait fish that they did not notice our lures. The tuna were fun to watch, though. They would thrash the surface into a frenzy, and as we approached with the boat they would sound and within a minute would surface four hundred yards away and start feeding again. Their apparent speed was impressive, and gave thought to the fight they would put up if hooked.

Each day the fishing improved and my stomach for the sea settled. By the end of the week we were capable, experienced fishermen. I still recall the buzzing sound of the reel when a kingfish took a lure on the troll and the excitement while looking into the depths to see what emerged after the fight.

Six years later I would return to Bucknor Banks with my cousin Robin. We had no car, so we hitchhiked from Kingston to Montego Bay and then took a country bus to Mosquito Cove, walking the final three or so miles to Sunnyville. Looking for someone to take us out to sea, we contacted people in Jericho and one man said that he was a fisherman and would take us out. With no car we could not take the outboard motor. We walked that evening to the boat shed at Mosquito Cove. The 'fisherman' brought along a young boy as an assistant to pull the anchor and we paddled out of the cove, dip-netting bait. By the time we reached the cove mouth, the waves were kicking up to about eight feet and the fisherman became seasick. Unable to navigate or to help us row, he lay helpless in the bilge the entire night. Somehow we found the banks and for some unknown reason I did not get seasick. We had never before caught so many fish, but because the sharks started taking our fish and because the fisherman declared that he would surely die unless he returned to land, we were forced to pull anchor and find the narrow cove entrance in the pitch black night. Somehow we were able to find our way with no help and I often wonder at our wonderful stupidity, to even venture out without a motor, much less a proper fisherman guide. The Lord must truly protect the stupid.

Getting back to shore was just the start of our difficulties. We were faced with an eight hundred foot climb with fishing gear and over one hundred pounds of fish. Somehow we made it to Jericho where we sold most of the fish and on the return journey to Kingston were able to buy airplane tickets from Montego Bay.

Few fishing places are as alluring to me as Bucknor Banks, the scene of my first sea experience. I wonder if there are still fish there or if it has suffered from the overfishing that has affected the rest of Jamaica's waters. I plan to find out some day.

Chapter eight

Gregory

The Lopez family hailed from the red hills of St. Catherine, about two miles southwest of Guanaboa Vale on the road that connects Guanaboa Vale with Bushy Park. They owned a small farm of thirty acres but for some unknown reason did not actually farm. I think that our families must have originally met at church in Spanish Town.

Carl Lopez was a ruddy-faced former seaman who had crewed on merchant ships during the war, when he moved his family from Kingston to the farm. By the early 1950s, he decided to give up the seagoing life and got a job as a shipping clerk at Hardware & Lumber, a Kingston shipping and hardware business. He was an argumentative fellow who always had an opinion about things that he had no real knowledge of and would enter into heated discussions with my dad about the correct way to grow a particular crop, despite never having grown anything. Mrs. Lopez was a tall, pleasant lady, a descendant of the Germans who had settled in the Ulster Spring area of Trelawny in the mid-1800s. She would just sit there while Carl argued and became more red-faced. They had four children, John, Gregory, Janet and Christopher, all born between 1940 and 1948, but Gregory was the one who stood out. He was not only tall for the times at about six feet six inches, but was also an interesting, resourceful and generous individual.

By about 1958, the three older Lopez children had got jobs in Kingston and travelled the twenty or so miles daily in their 1932 Austin motor car. On their way home, they would often stop by our farm so that Mr. Lopez could continue to irritate my dad with his theories on farming and we got to know the children fairly well as we sat there listening to the discourse. The oldest son, John, soon married Erol, the oldest daughter of A.U. King, then mayor of Spanish Town and local butcher of Kitson Town, after which he was no longer a part of the visits.

Gregory was mechanically gifted and now I realize that he could visualize how even the most complex things worked, particularly mechanical devices. He would fix anything that was broken in our household even if he was not asked and with that sort of talent soon turned his hand to fixing up old cars, a task that was only later to gain widespread interest elsewhere. The first car he restored was a 1948 MG-TD, a rare and much sought after English sports car. I recall him towing it up the hill just after he bought it for ten pounds and I thought that there was no way he could ever get it working. He stripped it down to the chassis and completely rebuilt it, making parts where he could not buy them. It took a full year, and when it was finished he drove it down to show my dad, beaming with pride. The sale of that car earned enough to buy a replacement for the old Austin family car, which was then stripped of its body and turned into a hot rod. I was visiting the Lopez home a year or so later and ended up getting a ride in the hot rod. It bore no resemblance to its former self and all that remained was a chassis, an engine and a bench seat. Gregory took me for a spin down the unpaved red dirt road, with me holding a gallon bottle of gasoline high above my head to gravity feed the engine while he took off in a squeal of red dust. Its souped-up engine bereft of muffler, the hot rod roared down the road, hitting every bump hard without the weight of the body to tension the suspension, while I held on to the dashboard for dear life while the gasoline splashed all over. To round things off, he drove by Mr. Laidlaw's gate and spun the car in a cloud of dust. Mr. Laidlaw had three beautiful daughters and this got their attention before their dad came out and hustled them back inside.

Gregory wrecked his family's new car in the summer of 1961 when our cousins Steve and Dawne were visiting. In our parents' absence, we took off with Gregory to find mangoes at Bendon, the second farm my dad owned. On the way back home, he managed to roll the car three times with seven of us in it at Mr. Ho'on's gate. He was the only one banged up, with a bump on his head at least half the size of his head. Naturally, he saw no need for a doctor, just some ice. He had a cut on his knee and stitched it himself with a needle and thread from mom's sewing kit. He was a tough character who never sought a fight but would never back away from one.

A few years later he bought a Vespa scooter and that became his ride to work. One day while on his way home he saw a man snatch a lady's purse, making his escape on a bicycle. Gregory rode up alongside the crook, held onto the bicycle seat and yanked it to the ground. He dismounted as the crook faced him off and he later insisted that he had been watching the crook's right hand but he turned out to be left handed. He left the hospital that night with his arm in a sling and a severe stab wound to his right shoulder, but the thief had to be admitted to hospital. Gregory arrived at our house later that night, somehow managing to ride the twelve miles with his left arm in a sling, working the scooter controls with the other arm.

For his next project, he was to attempt to be the first to take a vehicle to Blue Mountain Peak and for this he planned the restoration of an old World War II-era Willys Jeep. The elevation of the Peak is 7,400 feet and it was served by a bridle trail that was seven miles from the last road suitable for a four wheel drive vehicle. Winston Churchill had traded access to Jamaican and other West Indian island bases to the USA during WW II in exchange for Liberty ships, and bases were set up by 1941, fully equipped with American equipment. Soon after the war, the bases in Jamaica were closed and the equipment sold as military surplus, but two Willys Jeeps were never sold.

They remained on blocks from 1946 until 1961 when Gregory bought them for his project. We had gone on a reconnaissance hike to Blue Mountain Peak earlier that year with the specific mission of measuring the narrowest points on the bridle trail. Parts of the trail turned out to be nine inches narrower than the track of the Jeep. The solution was simple, though – part of the restoration would be to narrow the jeep by nine inches. This meant cutting the chassis, the axles and the body. Parts for WW II-era US Army surplus Jeeps were simply unavailable, so the two Jeeps were turned into one, and where parts were bad on both, Gregory built them himself. It was a difficult trip, and they did not get to the peak mainly because they ran out of time; broken suspension parts had to be removed and taken back to civilization by foot to be welded. Although he did not make it to the peak, the expedition was well covered in *The Daily Gleaner*, occupying the entire centrespread, with pictures and an interview with Gregory and his buddies about the trip.

Gregory's job at an appliance store gave him access to a full machine shop, and he would often tinker with ideas after work. He made a number of fine articles and one day showed up at our home with a very well made hunting knife that he had fashioned from a car's leaf spring blade, with circular strips of leather for the handle. The next thing he built was a spear gun for me to use in the irrigation canals surrounding our property. It was very effective and I was amazed that he had been able to make it without a commercially-made model at hand to observe or imitate.

Then there was the time when Gregory found an unexploded three inch mortar round at the army range at Green Bay and decided to see how it worked. He proceeded to cut it open with a hacksaw, hoping that holding it underwater while cutting would stop any sparks from triggering it. He somehow survived and proudly showed us how he then dug out the explosive with a wooden spoon and how he planned to use it to set off an explosion using a large firecracker as a detonator.

On weekends he could always be found working on some device or other. He became a jack of all trades and was to become an excellent electrician, plumber, welder and appliance repairman. He tuned and repaired all my family's cars.

By the mid 1960s, Gregory decided to plant crops on his dad's farm. Farming in Jamaica carries the high risk of crop theft so he applied for a firearm license. He bought a .22 single shot rifle and, as with everything else, became an expert marksman. To show off his prowess, Gregory would go bird shooting for doves. All the other hunters had pump-action shot guns, but he claimed to get more birds with the single-shot .22. I was by that stage a good shot myself, having learned to shoot with the cadets, and was at his home one Sunday sharing the rifle at target practice. Gregory was always bored with the mundane so to liven things up proceeded to convinced his younger brother to stand twenty yards away, in profile, with a lit cigarette in his mouth. Inspired by some cowboy movie, Gregory then used the .22 to shoot the burning tip of the cigarette. He did this twice that day despite our yelling at him to stop. I guess that if he lived in America he would have been a redneck.

Besides the rifle, the Lopez family had a pack of mongrel dogs on the property to protect the household. These dogs, numbering about a dozen, were not always locked up and anyone entering the yard, or for that matter passing on the road, took their life in their hands. Mr. Lopez had an old horse that he wanted to sell and put word out in Kitson Town. A potential buyer arrived early one Saturday morning to see the horse and, not being from the immediate area, he did not know of the dogs. After shouting "Hold dog!" a few times just in case, a normal Jamaican tactic, he walked up the driveway to the house. The pack attacked halfway up the driveway and the poor fellow sought altitude to escape. Unfortunately the only nearby tree he could find to climb was a tall banana tree, but any port in a storm. He hugged the slippery trunk and tried to scoot up out of range of the leaping dogs. Unfortunately banana trees tend to slough off outer layers under weight and, screaming for help the whole time, he slowly slipped within range of the fangs. The largest of the mutts finally managed to get a jaw full of his exposed crotch just before Gregory came to the rescue. The man, screaming in pain, immediately dropped his trousers to survey the damage only to be sternly admonished by Mr. Lopez; "I have young daughters, sir, dress yourself!" The irony of the event is that he bought the horse that day but could not ride it home.

Even after my parents moved to Kingston in 1968, Gregory was still a regular visitor. By 1972 I was married and had moved to my own place. Gregory was also married and living in a cottage he had built himself on the family farm. That July, making plans for my youngest sister's wedding, mom decided that the reception would be at her house in Cherry Gardens, Kingston. The house had a large backyard lawn so it was decided that tables and chairs would be rented for the hundred or so guests. Gregory was called in to arrange the lighting. On the day before the wedding, as I was driving down the road to my parents' place, I spied Gregory on the roof of the house standing next to the electric company mains supply. My brother-in-law Gordon asked him what he was doing up there and in vintage Gregory style he said "I think the electric company should help with this wedding!" while attaching wires to the live wire upstream of the electric meter. This convinced me that he had a bit of Anancy in him, in addition to superb mechanical abilities he had so capably shown throughout his then young life. This trait was not unusual, though, and was a part, some more and some less, in the character of most middle class Jamaican's of that era.

Jamaica lost many talented people in the 1970s as the government of the day struggled to bring the masses of the people up the economic ladder. To finance this, they targeted the middle class. The Prime Minister, Michael Manley, perhaps in frustration at the talent drain, famously said that there were five flights a day to Miami and those who did not like what he was trying to do were welcome to take one. Many did. Feeling unwelcome under the socialist government, the Lopez family migrated in the mid-1970s. They settled in the Toronto, Canada area and Gregory settled well into a job as an appliance installer with

Sears. He was a character with many talents and I often wonder what a great engineer he would have made if he had had the opportunity to go beyond primary school.

Chapter nine

The Tradesmen & Itinerant Sellers

In the days before the Internet – we did not even possess a telephone for all the years we lived on Featherbed Lane – all services and goods were purchased at arm's length. I can recall tinsmiths, wheelwrights, blacksmiths, carpenters, fence men and pit diggers all arriving on foot and inquiring if any jobs were needed. The farm had but a few permanent workers, usually those associated with herding and milking the cows or tending the pastures and any need for specific skills was periodically filled by these wandering tradesmen. My all time favourite was Mr. Grey the fence man.

The Fence Man

Mr. Grey was a middle-aged man of large size and gentle nature who tolerated the endless questions of a pre-teen. His job was to plant fence posts and string barbed wire and his tools were two steel crowbars for heavy digging, a cutlass, a sturdy cooking pot and a hammer.

He would work on the farm about once per year to replace sections of fencing on the various cow pastures but would pass by every week to see if any emergency repairs were needed. The hardwood fence posts were generally purchased from the western parish of St. Elizabeth and arrived as a truckload of six-inch diameter, seven-foot long posts. Termites or the odd rogue cow would routinely destroy the wooden posts, so constant maintenance was necessary for the many miles of fence that a sixty-five acre farm required.

Mr. Grey almost always arrived atop his little grey donkey, sitting partially side-saddle, with his cooking pot and supplies in the hamper and his tools slung alongside the flank like a cowboy's rifle. He invariably whistled as he rode, with one knee draped around the horn of the hamper. Dad would meet with him to agree on the job and the cost for the day and he would then jiggle off on the fast-stepping donkey to the job site.

I would often arrive at his jobsite at about 11.00 a.m. on a Saturday morning at about the time he took a break to set up his pot. By this time he would have a small wood fire going between large stones and would be kneading moistened flour and cornmeal into large dumplings. After adding these to the pot, he would then throw in a couple of green bananas and a side of salted cod. I don't know where the water came from, but assumed that it was from a nearby irrigation trench. He would go back to digging postholes as the meal cooked, and I can recall how he grunted as he methodically plunged the crowbar into the ground. The heavy clay was tough to remove and he would circumscribe little circles at the bottom of the hole with the flattened end of the crowbar, about five inches deep each time, and then use his hand to work the section of moist clay out the hole. It took about a half-hour to complete each hole, and as each section of clay was tossed out, I would pick it up and inspect the layers of different colours. The top six or seven inches were crumbly, dark brown topsoil, and this would immediately change to tight clay, starting with a light brown progressing to a pinkish-red. He would then select a post and stand it in the hole, tamping soil around it with the butt end of the crowbar while eyeballing it, much like a golfer lining up a putt, to make sure that it was vertical.

He would take a lunch break at midday and we would sit down under a nearby guango tree to a meal that at that time seemed quite exotic to me. He shared freely of his meal, and would regale me with stories of Br'er Anancy and Tucuma. Anancy was a sly character based on a spider whose only redeeming trait was his cunning. These stories had their roots in slavery and African culture. I never figured out what manner of creature the sidekick Tucuma was but heartily enjoyed the stories and eating rough food with dirty hands with this gentle giant of a man. Mr. Grey was a 'Panama Man', one of the thousands of Jamaica workers that provided the labour to build the Panama Canal. He told me that he had spent one year in Panama in 1913, where his main job had been moving the tracks of the trains that were used to remove the rubble. The tracks were re-laid each time a new 'step' in the famous canal was cut into the mountainside.

As the line of posts grew, he would arrive at a corner, and that called for a bigger post with diagonal braces. The braces were notched into the main post about half way up and sat in shallower holes dug on the diagonal. The barbed wire was attached first, to the end or corner post, and then one of the crowbars was used as an axle to play out the string from a spool. He would use the other crowbar as a lever to stretch the string, about twenty yards at a time, hold it taut with one hand and drive staples in with the other. No gloves, no shoes, no problem. Mr. Grey would never do any more or any less than agreed, and after he had stretched the four strings of barbed wire, he would wait for 'Busha' to come and inspect the work.

Though he had never attended school as a boy and could not read, Mr. Grey was numerically very literate. As dad inspected the work and calculated the payment, he would jump right in to correct any error in my father's math. The details would then be entered in Busha's workbook for payment on Friday afternoon. There was either great trust or great memory at work on Fridays. I suppose upon reflection that it was mostly trust, and that there was a symbiotic relationship that had established itself after the abolition of slavery one hundred and twenty years earlier. There was then a mutual respect between labour and boss that was to suddenly dissolve into mistrust in the mid-1970s.

I don't know what became of Mr. Grey after the farm was sold in 1968. My parents had always encouraged thrift and even started savings accounts for some of the full-time workers, but the tradesmen were independent contractors and were on their own. I suppose that, like all other aging men during that time, he would have been taken care of by the extended family that lived in the same tenement yard. These 'yards' were populated by up to thirty or so individuals of all ages, and those that had food would often make a community pot and share with those that would otherwise go hungry.

The Wheelwright

Other than a twenty-five horsepower tractor, the only means of carrying supplies on the farm was animal power. There were three mules and my sister's old horse 'Silver Mane' at Browndale. The mules were used in a variety of ways but mostly to pull carts of various types. The milk cart was a rubber-wheeled box-body about five feet wide and seven feet long. It had two parallel wooden shafts attached to the front, between which the mule was harnessed. This cart was used to haul milk churns to Spanish Town for the retail trade, and less famously, to haul Chris and me to high school, at least until we were teased senseless by the students who didn't even have a cart.

The wheelwright worked on all the other carts, those with steel-rimmed, wooden wheels, and his job was to replace the wood when the wheel fell apart. This was a laborious exercise; first he would hack out sections of hardwood into eighths of a complete circle and chisel out holes, on the inner side of each section, for two inch spokes. This was all done with an adze and with no apparent template except for the occasional dry fitting to the steel rim. The hub was then fashioned from an even harder wood, more spoke holes were chiseled, and then two steel bands were heated and placed over the hub to hold it all together. An iron sleeve was then hammered into the central hole. The spokes were precision fitted, after which all the wooden pieces were in place except for the rim. The old rim, five or six feet in diameter, about three inches wide and a quarter inch thick, was cleaned of the old wood and placed entirely into a roaring fire. This caused it to expand, and while it was red-hot, it was removed with a pair of tongs and the wooden sections friction fitted on its inner diameter. Water would then be thrown on the wheel. After the clouds of steam cleared, one had a tight fitting outer wheel that pulled the entire assembly tightly together. It was amazing to me then, and even more so now, the amount of hard labour, skill and craftsmanship that went into such a simple device. I wonder what became of the wheelwrights after the development of modern tyres put these skilled tradesmen out of work

The Tinsmith

Mr. Smith always arrived atop a small donkey-powered cart, usually accompanied by a young apprentice. The back of the cart was filled with his tools of trade and supplies of galvanized steel sheeting, some in rolls and some in sheets. There were pots of solvent, rolls of solder, tongs, pliers, hammers and an assortment of odd-looking instruments he would use to seam, bend and work the steel sheets.

Like all other tradesmen, he seemed to work a circuit of the farms and businesses in the area and would invariably show up on the third Monday of every other month. This was the era before plastics and it seemed that every container was made of sheet metal. The chimney for the old wood stove in our kitchen was a Rube Goldberg contraption of tubing, guy wires, bends and a silly looking pyramid-shaped cap that I recall looking surprisingly like the hat on the tin man in the Wizard of Oz. It seemed to always need repair. The galvanized steel milk churns, with capacities ranging from three to ten gallons, were often roughly handled and either a handle would come loose or a hole would form. These would need to be soldered. Mom seemed to have an unlimited need for little round cans with fitted lids for making and shipping Christmas puddings to all her sisters in distant lands. These cans were made entirely by hand by the tinsmith.

The day would start with the normal informal contract of work, and the apprentice would start up a small wood fire in the backyard. The andirons would be placed in the fire to heat while Mr. Smith (in retrospect I am not sure if this was actually his name, as the painter had an equally descriptive name - Mr. Dauber; I suspect nickname followed profession) pulled up his stool next to his anvil. Sitting astride the anvil he would hammer the sheet into whatever shape the job called for. The shears were angry looking big brothers to mom's scissors and it was amazing how they could cut through metal. The hammering would be a staccato of blows with every third strike hitting the bare anvil as the work was turned, so as not to slow the tempo.

To us youngsters, Mr. Smith seemed very old, but he was probably about sixty-five years old. He was heavyset with a grey beard and a curiously mottled, light brown complexion. He always sported a floppy hat and drab leather overalls. He constantly smoked hand-rolled cigarettes and would stop his work every once in a while to cut tobacco from a roll of jackass rope (tobacco leaves twisted into a coil about three-quarters of an inch in diameter). He would slice the tobacco in the manner of a chef fine-cutting vegetables, heap it into a little pyramid, pour this into a small sheet of paper and make his little cigarette. He would use the andiron to light the cigarette and then, squinting his eyes against the smoke, continue hammering while he hummed between puffs.

Pie tins and chimneys were made in the same way. After the sheet was rolled on the anvil to the correct circumference, a groove was made with a small chisel into the two opposing sides of the circle and these were interlocked and hammered shut. For pie tins, the circular bottom section was groove-fitted with the sides, the groove hammered shut and a bead of solder melted into the seam. The pie tin tops were made from a strip of metal sheeting about a half inch wide soldered to a circular top. In retrospect, I wonder about lead poisoning from the beads of solder, which in those days was mostly lead. The individual sections of chimney were beveled so that one end would fit into the other and the seam was soldered closed. The andirons were evil looking things with the shape of a hammer, but with a wedge-shaped end in place of the claw. They would be heated red-hot in the fire and would quickly melt and work the solder. I don't recall Mr. Smith using any measuring device. Nonetheless, everything was a perfect fit.

My brother and I learnt the basics of melting metals by watching Mr. Smith and were ourselves to experiment by melting the lead from old car batteries in an old motorcar hubcap over an open fire. The result of this experiment became the discus for our front yard games.

The Carpenter

Mel the carpenter was reed thin, in his mid 40s and a known drunkard. If it were not for mom, dad would have never hired Mel, considering him a terminal drunk and no good. He was a competent carpenter in his brief sober periods and my mother persevered with him in the vain hope that she could somehow cure him by constantly berating him about his drinking. A love-hate relationship persisted for the entire ten-year period that he did work for the family.

Mel was not one on the circuit and dad knew that he could always find him at the corner rum shop whenever he needed him. Mel never arrived on the appointed day and he never finished the job on time, much like the modern-day computer programmer.

He would show up on a dilapidated bicycle with a toolbox strapped to the carrier behind the seat. The saw and level were too long for the box, so they were tied to the bar of the bicycle. He would dismount while still moving, utilising the unusual maneuver of throwing his right leg over the handlebar. That forward dismount allowed him to avoid the toolbox which must have caught his leg in the past and brought him down. The dismount was the equivalent of throwing one's right leg forward over the horse's head, timing the slipping of the left foot from the stirrup and landing on both feet at the same time. This would have been difficult for a sober man, but to his credit Mel always seemed to pull it off without incident.

The array of tools he possessed was fascinating to me as a child. He had a couple of hand planes that he used to smooth the rough edges of cut lumber, creating the most wondrous curled strips of wood shavings as they were pushed along the grain of the wood. I was never quite sure what decided when it was done but I loved playing with and smelling the clean shavings. The wood drill was hand driven, and had a freely rotating three-inch circular wood pressure plate that he would press with his chest while he worked the drill with both hands. The drill went down from the pressure plate as a steel shaft that branched into a squared-off 'U' shape in the middle. On the working end, it had a bit-holder that was rotated to hold different sized bits. The bits were corkscrew shaped with sharpened screw tips and made amazing progress as they bit into even the hardest wood. There were also two saws, one large and tapered and the other shorter and square, for cutting miters and rabbit joints. The other fascinating tools were the chisels. He had perhaps five of different widths, and before he started work each day he would sit down with an oilstone and hone the edges of all the chisels and the plane's blade. This consisted of pouring a few drops of oil on the stone and working the edges of the metal in single strokes away from his body. I wondered how this could sharpen anything as tough as steel, but it worked well and he could slice a piece of paper with the edges when he was finished.

The first day was for estimating cost and material and, if approved, it was my dad's job to go buy the wood and other material. The lumberyard in Spanish Town was one of the only mechanized factories around and it was a marvel of loud buzzing circular saws used to cut trees into lumber, mounds of sawdust and the most exquisite scraps of wood that we were allowed to take home and make into toys. This was all tropical hardwood, no pine or fir, and was dense and heavy. Dad would have the selected pieces of lumber tied to the roof of the car and would carry them home that way. The hardware store was an old-fashioned country store that bore no resemblance to a modern hardware. It was a wonder of tools, nails by the pound, cement and other supplies. It was run by Edgar Fonseca, a descendant of Portuguese Jews who came to Jamaica during the inquisitions of the seventeenth century. Uncle Edgar was by then in his early seventies and had earlier married his cashier, Aunt May. May was a rotund St. Elizabeth 'poor white' woman who had the aggressive vocabulary of a sailor and was perhaps thirty years his junior. Edgar sat in a wire mesh cage and could have come right out of *The Saturday Evening Post* with a green eyeshade and long-sleeved shirt, cuffs held half way up his arm by rubber bands around the biceps.

After he was told that the material was there, Mel would arrive and, juggling this job with others in true carpenter style, would always take two weeks too long.

The Fish Vendor

A long, clear whistle blast announced the fish vendor as he rode by the gate at Featherbed Lane on his rounds from Old Harbour Bay, fifteen miles away. He did not actually catch any fish; he bought them at boat side and retailed them to customers along the route. He rode a bicycle with a wicker basket strapped to the back carrier, much in the style of the carpenter's toolbox. The basket was lined with a crocus bag, packed with ice and contained about twenty pounds of fish. The crocus bag lining folded over the top and held a three-chain scale.

If we needed fish the maid would be told to listen out for the whistle and to shout for him to stop as he rode by. He would then coast to a stop and start the process of unbundling the scale and uncovering the fish. We would eagerly encircle him as mom or the maid would point out the fish that they wanted. The majority of the fish would be snappers, though there would also be multi-coloured parrotfish and silvery kingfish. Fresh from the sea, the fish were all gleaming in bright colours with the yellow, green or pink of the kingfish contrasting with all the other shades of red. Mom would buy fish about once per week, twice at Lent, and tended to buy red or yellow tail snapper and a few steaks of kingfish. Then there was the traditional price negotiation with the seller throwing his hands heavenward, claiming eternal poverty and finally a price would be agreed and he would set off on his route. This ritual was repeated at every sale.

This same fisherman, Mr. Jones, plied the route for the entire period of my childhood. He had a happy customer base that would continue to buy fish from him even though fish could be bought at the market in Spanish Town. He never seemed to age and never lost his sense of humour during all of this time, but his was a vanishing trade as the motor took over from the bicycle and as the supermarket cut into his business.

The Tree Man

Every once in a while, dad needed a tree to be taken out and given the cost of the alternative, a Caterpillar tractor, the tree man was always the low bid for taking down and removing the stump of single trees. For larger jobs, like when one pasture was converted into a cane field and about ten very large guango trees had to go, then the tractor won that bid.

The main weapon of the tree man was his mattock, an axe with a narrow-width hoe on the reverse side. Depending on the size of the tree, he would dig a circular trench around it, cutting the roots as they were uncovered. The mattock was ideal for the job as it simply had to be rotated to move from digging to chopping. In this clay soil, all the roots usually grew horizontally just under the surface but logwood trees had a habit of thrusting a taproot deep into the clay which made them particularly difficult to bring down. As the trench grew deeper, he would climb the tree and chop off the limbs to one side to unbalance the weight so it would fall in a predetermined direction. If it was a large guango, it would take two or so days of heavy work just to get it down and then he had the even harder task of chopping off the remaining branches while it was on the ground.

The 1951 hurricane devastated the trees on the farm, felling scores of tall coconut trees and pushing over many guangos. Although the smaller logwoods, fruit trees and cashaw all seemed to survive with only a few branches blown off, the overall scene was depressing to dad but meant a lucrative job for the tree man. First he was paid one shilling each to cut up the fallen coconut trees and pile them into a heap for burning. Also, the large guangos had to be de-limbed, after which dad would chain the large trunks to our small Ferguson tractor and work the remaining roots free of the ground. This was a major exercise and I can still see the tree man sitting astride a huge guango limb hacking into it with a cutlass while the sound echoed across the field.

The Obeah Woman

Mother Ritti was an obeah woman. Born Ritinela Walters, she lived on Job Lane, next to the Bog Walk-Spanish Town Railway line, in a large walled compound resplendent with coloured flags atop fifty-foot tall bamboo poles – the mark of obeah. Her path was to cross that of our family when she bought my dad's 1948 Ford.

Obeah was a time-honoured profession in Jamaican society, inherited from African roots. The shaman, witch doctor, voodoo man and the medicine man all wrapped up into one, the obeah men and women relied on guile, superstition and a bit of chemistry to keep the customers coming in. They would deal with all manner of ailments, using bush medicine to cure diseases, as well as providing other services, such as pushing pins into effigies to punish an enemy, and powders that would tell if a partner was cheating if instructions were followed to add water at midnight on the full moon - if it turned purple, then the boyfriend was cheating. The irony is that although they were among the most prosperous people in rural Jamaica, their customers were drawn from the very poorest. They themselves were superstitious.

Mother Ritti was famous for her large and imposing figure and for her apparent control over the populace of a large area of rural St. Catherine. Her closest competitor lived on Mount Rosser, about 20 miles away, and from her walled Job Lane compound she held royal sway over the flatlands surrounding Spanish Town. She was at the same time feared, trusted, hated and respected.

I well recall the visit of Mother Ritti and her entourage one Saturday in 1959. She arrived in a taxi in response to word that dad put out that our car was for sale. After a cursory glance at the car, she pronounced it adequate, paying half the three hundred pound asking price from a wad of five pound notes that she pulled from a draw-string cloth bag tucked between her ample breasts. Not expecting a sale that quickly, dad was initially undecided about accepting the offer, but soon relented, enticed by the cash sale. Time did not allow for the formal title transfer to take place then, and Mother Ritti set off with her driver, promising to return on Monday to pay the balance and sign the transfer.

Little did we know, but Mother Ritti was also a ganja trader – a good second profession for an obeah woman. The police stopped by the morning after the sale to say that they had stopped the car in a roadblock on Old Harbour Road and found it packed with ganja. They were backtracking to find the owner, since the plates had been switched. Apparently the driver would not say, and Mother Ritti had quickly announced that the car had been stolen. Dad escaped suspicion because of his prominence in the society.

In their attempt to find all the packages of ganja, the cops had taken out all the seats and door panels. Dad was furious that his car had been used in this way, putting suspicion on his name, and was not interested in taking back the car. He instructed the police sergeant to return it to Mother Ritti, fully expecting her to honour her commitment to pay the balance on Monday. Monday came and went, but Mother Ritti didn't.

For the next month or so, dad tried everything he knew of to collect, to no avail. The police were a little afraid of this lady, perhaps with some apprehension that they may be burnt in effigy or something equally inconvenient, and would not act. Enter Dr. Richards.

Doctor Richards was a General Practitioner with offices in Spanish Town, and in his practice he not only met many of the poor people in the area, but also knew the culture intimately. He was from a humble background himself, and in a strange twist, Mother Ritti was a competitor for his patients. As is the custom in rural Jamaica, people visited friends frequently, and one Friday night while the Richards family visited Browndale, a conversation got started about the ganja, the debt and Mother Ritti. Dr. Richards decided that he would take on the challenge of getting the money from mother Ritti, and, with dad's permission, plotted his strategy. The very next Monday, Mother Ritti arrived and paid dad the balance.

Dr. Richards had visited her on the Saturday and told her that he had had this strange dream that something terrible was about to befall her, and that made him apprehensive, so he wanted her interpretation. Dreams are the stuff of interpretation, one of the main revenue earners for obeah men and women. In the interview he revealed that he had a recollection, though dim, of the events leading up to the finale, and that she had owed someone some money and that this precipitated a cascade of events leading to her death. A week later, we were entertained by Doc Richard's recount of the 'reading'. He was a very animated man and acted out the session, then falling to the ground crying with laughter. Years later I was to see a television advert for a Jamaican fortune teller named Miss Cleo. It seems that the obeah act has been commercialized into yet another great Jamaican export.

Chapter ten

The Blue Mountains

From an early age I have been drawn to the mountains. I don't know why, perhaps it has to do with the solitude and majesty that man has always felt in their presence. Africa is about seeing Kilimanjaro and Mount Kenya and camping in their shadows just to watch the sun paint the icecaps in the pre-dawn hours. On my numerous Asian business trips, I always sought flights with routes that passed over Northern India and Southern Alaska just to see Everest or Denali or the huge volcanoes of Kamchatka soaring majestically above the cloud base. Normally an inveterate aisle traveller on local flights, a route over a mountain range would find me in a window seat, which must amuse fellow travellers that would rather have a beach cabin. I want a mountain cabin. I must see the Andes and the Mountains of the Moon.

My first recollection of Jamaica's Blue Mountains was in about 1950, where on visits to Grandma Kelly's house on Roosevelt Avenue in Kingston they seemed to dominate the North. I recall how cold and sweet the mountain-stream fed Kingston municipal water tasted when compared to the Rio Cobre water of Spanish Town.

Visiting Newcastle in about 1954 with Uncle Joe Kelly, I was amazed at the spectacle of looking down at clouds, the cold air and the serene beauty of the place. The smell of pine forests pervaded Hardwar Gap, two miles up the road from Newcastle. The sight of clouds flowing through and descending on the lee of the passes was surreal and we were in and out of clouds all day. We visited waterfalls and marvelled at the moss-covered tree ferns and the stunted, gnarled trees of the cloud forests had an enduring impact on me. The years that followed forged a love of these mountains that remains with me even now.

Newcastle at the time was a British army base that had been constructed on a buttress-ridge at an elevation of about 4,000 feet. Founded in the eighteenth century, the base had been continually occupied by rotating British Regiments, all of which left evidence of their sojourn through regimental Coats of Arms painted on the rock wall of the parade ground. The parade ground was mid-camp and about two acres with the barracks below and the Officers mess and Officers quarters perched above. The Commanding Officer occupied the loftiest residence surrounded by tennis courts and other accoutrements befitting the rank. Yellow fever was ravaging the Western world at the time and the British, knowing that the risk diminished with altitude, built the camp to preserve the lives of their troops. They had no idea that mosquitoes were the cause, and that there were no bugs at Newcastle.

In 1960 I was fortunate to return to Newcastle, this time as a cadet. The Army and Air Cadet force in Jamaica was set up in the high school system to teach discipline and leadership to male students, starting at about age fifteen (though I was only thirteen when I joined). It was a military program run by the army and the annual camps closely resembled the everyday activities in those institutions. The journey started with a train ride from Spanish Town to Kingston. Lugging a suitcase with two weeks supply of uniforms, boots and lots of anticipation, it must have been the first time that I was on my own. A bus ride from the train station to cadet headquarters brought the St. Jago High School cadets to the meeting point for the onward journey. I recall arriving at cadet headquarters to the news that the commander, a Major Wainwright, had earlier shot himself after being accused of being too familiar with young cadets. Major Mike Came, an English officer from the Hampshire Regiment, was given command, and in the coming years was to become my flight instructor and mentor.

The British regiment provided lorries (trucks) for the onward journey. Each barracks held a platoon, no hot water, no privacy and a lot of very cold air. I quickly realized that army life was not for me. The army bread baked for this damp, cold place was dubbed 'bulletproof' by the cadets – it had to survive for a week and the thick crust was apparently the protection needed. The parades, inspections and make-work were all intended to keep the troops busy, out of trouble and in line. This business of spending hours each evening spit polishing boots, gaiters and webbing, and cleaning brass buttons with a smelly liquid named Brasso, only to do it all over again the next day, seemed completely pointless to me. Years later I took the job of quartermaster sergeant of the school troop simply to avoid endlessly marching around.

I did love the shooting range though. Newcastle had a fifty yard range and at the tender age of thirteen, I was to use a .303 rifle for the first time. The tremendous bang and the recoil of the rifle, the smell of cordite and the clang of the bolt extracting the brass round were stimulating to a young boy.

Catherine's Peak, at an elevation of 5,000 feet, dominated the ridgeline that formed a backdrop to Newcastle. We were to climb this peak twice that year – the first time at 10:00 p.m. one night. After lights out, the entire barracks had a pillow fight and our NCO (the army non commissioned officer assigned to our barracks), a Corporal Rhooms, felt that we had enough energy to hike in our pyjamas to the peak. The next day we did the official hike, a distance of about two miles. All our senses were invaded by the haunting song of a small mountain bird, the solitaire, the exuberance of the fragrant ginger lily and the groves of sweet rose apples, and the masses of Spanish moss trailing from the tree ferns in the mist. The last few yards of the climb uncloaked a large, ugly radio tower. The panorama of the grand ridge of the Blue Mountains, seen for the first time across the Yallah's River valley, was an impressive sight to a young boy still discovering the world around him. I was hooked. This is what I wanted to do. I climbed the tower and just drank it all in. My senses were overloaded – the visuals of the mountains to one side and to the other the receding plains with their neat, rectangular sugar cane fields; the moaning of the wind through the gorse-like bushes on the peak; the faint curry-like smell of a grass that occupies much of the exposed, south-facing slopes in these mountains. To the north, beyond the mountains, a line of growing thunder clouds sailed, like schooners of old, across the cobalt blue sky.

My dad believed in making his boys tough, and in the summer of 1961 a hike from Gordon Town to Catherine's Peak was arranged. Gordon Town was about four or five miles by bridle trail (the old British Army trail) but about 3,500 feet below Catherine's Peak. My brother Chris, cousin Steve and friends Ronnie DuQuesnay and Morris Bruce made up the group. All of this was in preparation for climbing Blue Mountain Peak later that year which we knew was a tough, steep trail. Years later I was to hear a story of a young British officer's travails. Forced to frequently make the eight-mile march while stationed in Kingston in the 1870s, he requested a horse because of the difficulty of the trail. His commanding officer in England promptly turned his request down on the grounds that, as the crow flies, the map showed a distance of only 5 miles. "I, sir, am not a crow," was the reported response of my great-grandfather Patrick Kelly.

The tortured geology of the Blue Mountains, and in particular the southern range, was very different from the boring limestone hills in the central and western districts of the island. These were folded and fractured rocks, rich with minerals such as copper, iron, lead, zinc and large deposits of gypsum. Here there were rivers everywhere, tumbling over the black basaltic rocks and fuelled by the exceptionally high rainfall, over three hundred inches annually in the northeast, but an arid ten per cent of that a few miles further south at Port Royal.

In later 1961 we were to experience the full range of temperatures and rainfall that these mountains had to offer. Dad decided we were ready for a little more of a challenge and he drove us to Mavis Bank. On the southern flank of the Grand Range of the Blue Mountains, Mavis Bank was a small village in the coffee-growing district. The trail lead down to the Yallahs River, which flowed in a deep valley between the two ranges of the mountains. After a short but steep descent to the valley floor, we had to ford the Yallahs, then the Green River; we had to brace against the rush of the cold current rushing over impossibly smooth rocks of green, black and white marble, black basalt and green copper ores before climbing a considerable valley wall of about 2,000 feet elevation. After three or so miles, we arrived at Farm Hill Gap and there, revealed through the flowing mist, was the 7,400-foot mass of Blue Mountain peak set against an impossibly blue sky. This was a trial run and we were only allowed to continue for another mile or so to Whitfield Hall where John Algrove ran a hostel for trekkers to the peak.

The excitement that the view of the mountains raised in us was, in retrospect, a little amusing. We took off up a steep slope in the hope of getting to the top, realizing too late that not only were we miles away, but that we were two hundred feet up a dangerous slope of loose rocks with no apparent way down. John Algrove heard the shouts and was able to talk us down. Later, we retraced our steps to Mavis Bank where my parents patiently awaited the return of the four valiant adventurers.

At about 5,000 feet elevation and seven miles from the Peak, Whitfield Hall had survived perhaps a dozen hurricanes in its two hundred years. Dad had talked about a place named Torre Garda, a hostel he had stayed at in the 1920s when as a teacher at Jamaica College he would lead groups of schoolboys to the Peak. Torre Garda had apparently been destroyed, as no one in the area knew of it. The steep mountainsides produced the best coffee, flowers and thyme in the world. Growing at the entrance to the house was a blue gum tree, the largest of the Australian eucalyptus trees that must have been planted when the house was built. The tree rivalled those I was to see years later on the western slopes of Table Mountain in South Africa. It must have been over ten feet in diameter and two hundred feet tall. In the decade of the 60s we were to spend many memorable evenings at Whitfield Hall en route to the Peak.

Victory came in Easter 1962. We were deposited at Mavis Bank on a Friday afternoon, to be picked up on Sunday evening. Five of us, me, Chris, Steve, Mike Ffrench and Ronnie DuQuesnay set out with too much canned food, not enough rain gear or warm clothes and uncomfortable British Army surplus canteens and haversacks. It took us six or seven hours to hike the twelve miles.

The hike started in familiar territory, descending to and crossing the two rivers, then a painful climb up the northeast wall of the Yallahs valley. This first part was dusty and the steep hillsides were under intense cultivation with coffee, carrots and flowers. Three miles later we crested the valley wall and instantly it was cooler and damper at the 4,000-foot level at Farm Hill Gap. The Grand Ridge and the Caribbean Sea emerged and the vegetation was no longer mango and familiar dry lowland trees, but the Jamaica Cedar (similar to the excellent, slow-growing North American and Bermuda varieties). The trail was lined with yellow raspberry bushes, which in April were in full fruit and a delicious treat. The next half mile to Whitfield Hall was nearly all flat, running just below a ridge that was fully cultivated in temperate climate flowers.

About one hundred yards short of Whitfield Hall the cultivation turned to coffee, and we stopped in at the hostel for a drink and to fill our canteens and then slogged onward. By this time night was descending and we relied on the moonlight for staying on the trail. The next half mile was flat and paralleled a small stream. Rose apple trees covered the trail for the first time and, as the night descended, the cool temperatures set in. By this time the tins of milk and corned beef were pushing through the haversacks and the 40-pound weights were starting to work on the shoulder straps. We somehow got separated on this stretch, when Chris and Ronnie fell behind and took the wrong branch of the trail. We were able to shout to them and lead them back, but that set us back a half-hour at least. The fork signalled a steepening trail, and for the next mile or so we trudged along the side of a ridge covered with the most wonderful-smelling thyme and scallion. The local small farmers intensely cultivated these steep slopes for the fine quality of the spices produced, and it was sobering to think that we were panting and cussing on a trail that they had to use daily, even to take out their bulky produce.

The next mile was again tree-covered, and well signposted as a forest preserve. The trail again steepened and we were soon at Portland Gap. Portland Gap was the pass between Blue Mountain and Mossman's Peaks and about 5,000 feet in elevation. The wind howled through the gap, bringing a heavy mist. We pulled on our warm clothes and staggered on. This next section of the trail, known as Jacob's ladder (to some Devil's Ladder), consisted of 18 switchbacks that took the trail into a cloud forest. Here the most delicate, yellow-flowered snowdrops, mosses and other cool-climate shrubs bordered the trail. Tiny flowers abounded and the trees were shrouded in mosses and bromeliads. Thick, head-high bracken ferns populated the under story, and the tree ferns and stunted cloud forest trees grew no taller than about ten feet. The end of Jacob's ladder took us to the western ridge of the peak. After about another mile, the trail again spiralled counter clockwise around the base of the peak and approached from the north.

The routine at the time was that one had to pay a fee to use the lodge at the Peak. The Forest Department charged a princely five shillings and, in return, allowed you to use the lodge complete with its mattress-less bunks. Staggering onto a broad meadow from the north, we only realized that this was it when the lodge appeared in the starlight, brightly backlit by Kingston, 7,400 feet below. Yelling and hollering in what must have been relief, we were chastised by a sleepy Englishman who pushed his head from a pup tent to ask "I say, could you chaps keep it down out there!" Alas, there was no room in the lodge – there was good reason for the low fee for usage: they simply did not care if they overbooked. So, in the middle of the night, we had to find lodging all huddled together with about twenty other people in a wooden shack.

The morning was simply stunning. In the cold dawn we walked over to the steel pylon of the trig station on the Peak and watched the sun rise. The sun appeared to rise in the sea! It started out as a greenish globe, only faintly glowing and about four degrees below the horizon, image refracted by the atmosphere. Slowly moving upward, it took several minutes to touch the horizon. As it emerged, it shone brightly and revealed a wonderland of shadow, contour and colour. We decided that the smudge on the northern horizon must be the Sierra Madre Mountains of Cuba, 90 miles distant. The huge bank of clouds to the northeast must be a storm approaching. Stunted trees covered in moss told of the constant cloud cover. Masses of doctor birds (humming birds with impossibly long twin tail feathers, insolent personality and iridescent green beauty) flitted about with a bravado that belied their diminutive size.

This area was the flower capital of the island. The British, those unmatched plant lovers, descendants of Bligh of the Bounty who took their island's flora with them to the colonies, must have introduced the strawberries in the meadow. The hydrangeas on the south slope facing Kingston were enormous bushes with even more enormous flowers in blue and pink. We sat and watched the shadow of our mountain slowly pull inward across Kingston, flickering out the street lamps as day emerged. Marching away to the west beneath us were Mossman, High, Sir John and John Crow peaks. Catherine's Peak was a mere tit in the distance. Knife-ridged forests, probably never visited by man, ran away to the north towards Port Antonio and its twin harbours. The view to the east was somewhat obscured by East Peak, about a mile's walk away, and beyond that rose Sugarloaf Peak and Macka Sucka. The northern side of Sugarloaf hid the remains of Nanny Town, a sanctuary destroyed in the Maroon wars by the British two hundred years earlier. Chris and I were to visit Sugarloaf a few years later.

As we were running to East Peak through the bogs and moss and mist later that day, the weather changed. The bank of clouds slowly poured up the northeast slopes and, shooting overhead, arched quickly down the lee of the mountain. Visibility destroyed and temperature falling, we regretted wishing the clouds in. The upside of this was that most of the other hikers left, fading into the mist down the trail to Mavis Bank. Moving into the main lodge, we took control of the bunks and tried as best we could to stay warm. That night it stormed for over two hours. The lightning was continuous and the thunder simultaneous and deafening. We were literally in the belly of the storm. Fully expecting early mortality, we cowered in the dark and cold, expecting that if we survived, we would find the earth shredded.

The descent was harder than the ascent and, in a mad scramble downward, we took every shortcut that cut off the switchbacks. This is how kids had got themselves lost for days in these mountains. Finally the Green River appeared and we plunged into it, soaking away the mustiness and grime of two days. The slow, hand on knee plod up the slope to the road where my parents waited was the most difficult section of the hike. I picked up a beautiful piece of white and light green marble from the river and this ten pound rock became a part of my small rock collection. It was oily smooth and showed brilliant colour when wet. One day someone would find a way to mine the rocks from these mountains without destroying the place.

I was to return to Blue Mountain Peak some twenty times in the 1960s, though from a closer starting point. The road from Mahogany Vale was opened up to four-wheel traffic and we would contact John Algrove for a ride to Whitfield Hall. My cousin, Raymond Sowley, was to meet his first wife on one of these trips, when she helped him haul his considerable bulk to the Peak. I understand that the trail is now open to Jeep traffic all the way to Portland Gap, where there are now cottages – a bit of a shame as this has resulted in deforestation and overuse of the Peak.

A Free Range Boyhood

The family farm, Browndale, was a rectangle bordered on the east
by Featherbed Lane, on the south (separated by a grove of large
Logwood trees) by a property named Wick Hall and on the north and
west by the St. Dorothy irrigation canals. Fed from the Rio Cobre and
built in the 1870s, the canals provided irrigation water to most of the
central St. Catherine Plains, and a lifetime of memories for the Virtue
sons and daughters.

My mother had a fear of most types of physical danger and it was
understandable that as youngsters the presence of these canals was
guarded from us. This did not match up against her ability to let us run
almost at will and unsupervised from an early age, and she obviously
tried not to infect us with her fears. In later years she and Dad would
tell us stories of the early years when they had just moved to Spanish
Town; they would set a series of fishing poles with avocado bait and
they would catch dozens of river mullet. By the time we started fishing
in these canals, the mullet had virtually disappeared – apparently as

result of pollution from Bybrook sugar factory seven miles upstream in Bog Walk, and of the introduction of the voracious African perch (Tilapia) into the waterways.

My first awareness of the presence of the canals came in the mid-1950s; I discovered them when I was with the cow hands driving cattle to graze on a harvested rice field on Hampton Green property, which lay across from our farm. The Handals, the owners of that property, allowed Dad to graze these fields after each harvest and before the next planting. Returning home, I was eager to share this great discovery and, never for a moment thinking that we were not supposed to know of the existence, we approached the parents to quickly acquire fishing lines.

A 'canal man' who had twin responsibilities patrolled the canals, and one bank of the canal was held as a pathway from which he could carry out his duties. The first duty was ensuring that each contract user of water was supplied the correct number of 'yards' of water (I guess cubic yards per hour), and he did this by using an inch measure to check the depth of water flowing across the little waterfall at each feeder weir. If the water was flowing at the wrong rate, he would unlock the padlock from a large bunch of keys at his waist and change the flow by adjusting a screw gate. His second duty was seeing that the canals were not used illegally, which covered almost everything, from fishing to washing and swimming. The regular canal man, Mr. Green, was a kindly old man who never attended to the second of these duties. For this there was Catrick. His name lived in infamy and he was rumoured to have shot at least three hundred unlucky persons in his years of patrol. This obviously built his reputation in an English colony where authority was to be feared by all. He was a man of authority; he carried a gun and was not to be fooled with.

Our first fishing expedition on the banks of the irrigation canal was completely unsupervised and after digging up a bunch of earthworms, Chris and I went fishing in the smaller 'front' canal. I remember vividly when Chris hooked into an eel. He pulled it up onto the pathway and it coiled around the line and slipped the hook, heading for a coolie plum bramble. We pulled our Okapi penknives and gave chase. The eel was just about to slither into a mongoose hole when Chris pounced. The poor thing was taken home in noisy triumph, with 33 stab wounds. I don't think the cook wanted to tell us that eels were greasy and almost inedible as it would have disappointed us, so she steaked it and fried it up for us to decide. It was awful and we never took an eel home again.

For the first three or so years we confined our activities to fishing and to the smaller front canal, and by about 1960 Chris lost interest in fishing. My youngest sister, Mary, could be co-opted to accompany me on weekends and after school and we would ride on my Raleigh bicycle down the road to the point where the canal passed through a culvert under Featherbed Lane. There were two competing brands of British bicycles in those days and among us boys of the area we were always boasting that our Raleigh bicycles were better than the Rudge brand, in much the same way my dad and his brothers would boast that one's Studebaker was better than the other's Ford. Mary would sit on the cross bar and would hold the lines and the tin can with worms and I would pedal. She was becoming a real tomboy, but she didn't do too much fishing, and would just hang out and make idle conversation. Did I ever love her company. From the cistern downstream from the culvert, I would catch an incredible array of fish, including rockfish, sandfish, tilapia, eels and even the odd crayfish and shrimp. The shrimp were stupid creatures that would hang onto the bait even as you pulled in the line and the trick was to bring them to the surface slowly, and as soon as you could see them, flick them up onto dry land. On a good day in the mango season, when the shrimp population seemed to explode, you could catch dozens with the 'flick' method. The crayfish were more cerebral and needed a different technique – stealth. You would feel them slowly pulling the line and if you got too frisky they would let go. The trick was to use a special sized hook and to try and catch it around a toothy appendage that grew halfway up the non-moving side of the pincer. This type of crayfish had huge pincers, almost twice the body length, got to about a pound or two and was delicious to eat. There were other crayfish with thin pincers and a striped appearance, but those were almost impossible to catch.

In about 1960 we started using the canal to the back of the property. This was about twice the size of the front canal, about fifteen feet wide and somewhere between three and six feet deep. It ran the length of the property to the southern tip, named Point, and was much more interesting. Catrick patrolled this canal from his house a bit upstream, and whenever we were fishing we were constantly on alert. It was comical, since the canal path was used as a means of transit to Innswood Sugar Estate and there was a constant stream of people. If someone looked odd from a distance we would hop over the barbed-wire line onto our property until the threat passed. We used this canal for walking, for fishing, for snorkelling, spear fishing and for just plain romping in the water.

On many a Saturday, Uncle Will would drop off Dawne and Stephen on his way to work at Innswood sugar factory and we would all go for a walk. This would take Dawne, Steve, Rosie, Mary and me all the way to Point, then where the canal split into two branches we would follow the left branch, swing over the fence at Wick Hall property, walk through the pastures back to Featherbed Lane and return home by road. This was about a two-mile walk and as early teens we were never supervised nor were we ever bothered, even on the lonely stretches.

The borders of Browndale with the canal and with Wick Hall had mature forty-foot tall logwood trees that through the 1950s were roosting places for flocks of birds. Every evening at dusk there would be waves of white-winged doves leaving their feeding grounds in the rice fields and alighting in these trees. The sight and sounds of their arrival were unmistakable, and within thirty minutes there would be no tree branch with a bare spot. The flocks numbered in the tens of thousands, but the population seemed to collapse in a year or two and soon this was just a memory. By the early 1960s, DDT, habitat loss and hunting practically wiped out the population. This, combined with the later loss of nearly all the native fish in the canals, was an indication that even then chemicals and invasive species were impacting native wildlife.

The fishing here was good and my cousin Robin joined the fishing scene through most of the early sixties. We never wore shoes. We would dig up worms, climb over the thorn-filled area around the fence and get onto the canal bank. Mary or David would come along every once in a while and join in.

There was a section of the canal where it merged with a crystal-clear spring. Wearing goggles and flippers, we would dive into the canal and swim up the tributary, marvelling at the clarity of the water and the quantity and variety of fish and shrimp that clung to the grasses in the strong current. The fish in the spring were small so we spent our time shooting shrimp and crayfish with a small spear gun that was built for us by our friend Gregory Lopez.

Just upstream the converging streams stood our swimming hole. The swimming hole was about twenty feet wide and five to seven feet deep and on the far bank there were tall guango trees. We would climb the low branches and dive into the swimming hole and let the current take us downstream to a point where we could clamber out and do it again. We were often joined by local kids, none of whom wore any swim gear, and it gave us a chance to 'size up' the competition. After that we never had any desire to go trunk less.

Swimming was the most serious crime, so there was always a sentinel standing watch for Catrick. We would take turns, like a mongoose tribe on the African savannah with one member always on watch. In later years the swimming became romping and we would form warring factions, slinging mud and clay at each other. We would pick teams, and each team would choose a headland to hide behind. We would then lob shots of liquid mud at each other, trying to drop our shots over the opposition's headland. This would splatter the opposition and fill their eyes with mud. No one ever won these battles, but winning was not the point – having fun was. The canal was gradually widened through this excavation for mud bombs and we eventually had to move further downstream to avoid undermining the track. This activity continued until about 1963, even after Chris went off to University.

One other activity took us to the canal, and that was hunting and gathering. Waking at 5:00 a.m. on a Saturday, we would load our pockets with grape-sized stones, stick a homemade sling-shot in our back pockets and head out hunting. At this time of day all was peaceful, and all the birds were out and in full song. The air was fresh and the ground cool under our bare feet. The grass dripped with incredible amounts of dew, though it was noticeably absent under trees. One could be at peace with the world. The birds were at peace and had little to worry about from us, as our lack of success here was only to be outdone in later life in our quest for girls. But it was not about getting birds: it was about being out in the bush in the cool early morning.

The front canal ran through cultivated land, and here there were a number of bird habitats. The small migratory birds would tend to hang out in the taller trees, the ground doves and pea doves would be on open ground searching for seeds, and the mid-sized fruit eaters could be found in the bird cherry, jimbilin or guava trees. Bird cherries were seasonal and when they bore fruit, the whole tree would be loaded with sticky-sweet, blueberry-sized red fruit. Jimbilin is the sourest fruit made by God, but they are almost pucker-free just before they ripen – not unlike the North American persimmon. Guavas were my favourites, and the Hampton Green property held a large number of Spanish guavas, planted there by a previous owner, the reclusive Cuban John Valdez. Spanish guavas were large, pear-shaped fruit bred to make the most delightful guava cheese, and were excellent eaten ripe. The bluequits seemed to relish these and one could sneak up on them while they were neck deep in a ripe guava.

The 1870s dam that fed the canals was washed away by a flood in 1991 and for five years the canals ran dry. The dam has since been rebuilt and the canal system patched up, but it no longer holds the magic that it once did. The canals are still there, though civilization has stretched out into what was farm land and the houses now border the banks, destroying the peacefulness of the place. One can no longer just sit peacefully by the water and enjoy the sights and sounds of nature.

The upstream Bybrook sugar factory was closed but has been replaced with other polluters, mostly human.

The wonderful activities my brothers, my cousins and I engaged in led to a fair amount of bonding among us boys; it was carefree, illegal fun. It would have been interesting had Catrick collared any of us - dad was the Justice of the Peace that acted as a judge in what was called the Petty Sessions court in Spanish Town. He tried the misdemeanour cases such as cussing, riding a bicycle at night without lights and, yes, swimming in the irrigation canals.

Olympics in the front yard

The front yard of our home, Browndale was a bit over an acre, and was divided by the two irrigation ditches that ran parallel to Featherbed Lane. The section between the front of the house and the first ditch was the largest, and this was our Olympic field. It was here that we had our small golf green, our cricket pitch (until we broke one too many window panes in the house and had to move next door to the Handal's rice-drying barbeque) and our field events. It was here that the swing set was positioned, slightly off to the right, facing the road. This was to become Chris' folly.

Chris, Paul and our cousin Steve had come up with a series of events that were selected to hone skills for school sports day, to be followed shortly thereafter by Olympic fame. We all had feet of clay and became painfully aware of this at an early age, so track events were not for us. We settled on the field events. Scattered around the cow pen behind the house were a number of large, smooth, heavy and somewhat rounded black rocks. These basaltic rocks were originally from Rock River district in central Jamaica and must have spent many years in a riverbed being shaped into the perfect shot put. Not being familiar to the people in the area, it was felt by most that these strange rocks were formed by lightning strikes and they were given the name of "Thunder Stone". The stone was so dense that if hit with metal, it would take the sheen of the metal, being harder material.

We had to make our own discus; a car hubcap found on Featherbed Lane was placed on an open fire in the backyard and old motor car batteries were split open to reveal the lead plates. These were extracted, the acid washed off and the lead deposited into the open hubcap to melt. We had to skim off the oxides and other gunk as the lead beaded into molten droplets and ran to the bottom of the hubcap. When fully melted and skimmed free of gunk, we would tease the circumference into a sort of rim to remove any sharp edges, having learnt about a year earlier that sharp metal and digits do not work well together. Water would be used to douse the molten lead and it would be knocked out of the hubcap, taking the rounded shape on the bottom and a flat face on top. At about six pounds, this worked well as a discus.

We had weightlifting equipment in the backyard – the large, squared in cross section of an axle from one of dad's mule-drawn carts, weighing in at about 100 pounds, was used by the stronger cousins, and I remember the thrill the first time I was able to lift it above my head. The smaller, rounded axle from a lighter cart weighed about sixty pounds and was used for light workouts, or by the weaker cousins. It was an unspoken source of silent one-upmanship.

The weekends were a blur of activity. Morning was cricket or soccer or fishing illegally in the surrounding irrigation canals. Afternoons were spent at Bendon, the family's Red Hills property, hunting for mangoes, naseberries or cashews, or shooting birds with homemade slingshots. Some days we would work out on the weights and afterwards do some field events. Shot put records were about a fifth of the way out to the closest irrigation ditch, or about forty feet. The discus record was to that ditch, where the lead discus would often bury itself in the mud and defy retrieval. Most of the time, though, the discus landed on the hard lawn and required the periodic re-melt and re-shaping. Even with the rounding of the edges in the forging process, holding and throwing it was rough on the hands, and we would triple-fold newspaper to protect our hands. We never got very good at either event and we never put on visible muscle, but we kept trying because we had this continuing need to impress girls.

One Saturday in January, Teacher William's daughter Jasmine came visiting. She had been in my sister Geraldine's year at Friendship Primary School where her father was the tyrannical headmaster. Geraldine had been away at university in Canada and had returned for Christmas. I know it was after Christmas because the stem of the Christmas tree provided the equipment for our third field event – the javelin. Chris figured that since we weren't very good at discuss or shot put, perhaps we had secret muscles that might work better with a javelin, and after the Christmas tree was discarded, he used a cutlass to chop off the branches and sharpen the main stem, making it pointy so that it would fly right. It was a sight. The bark was peeling and the nubs of the branches were still visible. It was sappy and it was heavy.

Jasmine was a peach; as were all girls to a mid-teen boy. She was sitting on the swing chatting with Geraldine when Chris decided to break out the javelin and impress this older woman with his athletic prowess. The first throw went end over end and she pretended not to notice. The second wobbled out there, struggling to reach 100 feet. At this point, after trying and failing to impress, Chris's ego had taken enough of a beating, and he decided to give it his all.

He backed up to the garden bed next to the house and gathered himself for the task. He took off at a mad run, almost tripping over the dog, and with a loud grunt, let fly. The javelin flew true, slightly rotating along its axis, as it should. The girl looked up at the grunt, only to find herself in the bull's eye. She was frozen in disbelief, and when the Christmas tree found its mark halfway between her navel and her groin it threw her screaming to the ground in absolute agony. For some reason, probably coincidence, our parents were out.

I believe that this was when Chris had his medical epiphany. He ran over to this girl who was writhing in pain on the ground, with Geraldine screaming at us, and calmly said "Let me see it!" To this day we are not sure what Chris wanted to see, but give him the credit for wanting to help this poor girl whom he had grievously injured. Not for a second did we believe that he might have harboured any other thoughts, given the location of the blow.

This poor girl was laid out on the day bed on the verandah, and moaned even while Geraldine applied ice and tried to soothe her. Luckily the point of the javelin had been sufficiently blunted by earlier failed flights that it did not penetrate, but it left a huge black-and-blue mark and needed medical treatment.

We again closed ranks and rehearsed a likely story for the parents. Dad would have none of this and his remark, which still rings in our ears to this day was "You three sh---!" These are the strongest words we had ever heard this man utter.

The Day we cut the toe off

Summer days would find us with no inside activities. In these pre-television days, all our entertainment was self-generated. When we could not find much to do we would pull in the unfortunate younger sisters, making them the guinea pigs for our misadventures. One fine summer morning we decided to launch a boat and Mary, since she was smallest, was pressed into service as the captain. In addition to Steve and Dawne, our cousin from Kingston, Christine Kelly, was visiting and we managed to pull Mary away from paper dolls to a more interesting enterprise.

Living at least seven miles from the sea and at least two from the nearest river, the irrigation ditch in the front yard would have to do. Having neither boat nor the means to buy one, an old fifty gallon steel barrel was to be our seagoing vessel.

The blue team was set to work dredging the shallow irrigation ditch to flotation depth. The leader Chris set the task in motion, and Mary, Rosie, Christine and Dawne mucked out the canal, depositing the foul smelling mud onto the bank. The dredging ran from the culvert under the driveway to the water main that supplied the house, a distance of a hundred feet.

The red team, consisting of the other boys, had the task of cutting a boat out of the steel drum. Knowing that a boat should be somewhat longer than wide, these erstwhile youth cut the barrel lengthwise, leaving a vague canoe shaped vessel comprising about a third of the barrels diameter. The cutting tool was probably a cold chisel, since the gunwale of our boat was anything but smooth. No matter: Mary was tough and she was not supposed to touch the side anyway.

We awaited the parents' departure, on the theory that parents did not understand hydrodynamics and may find some flimsy reason to sink our plan. It was perhaps coincidental, but every misadventure that befell us in these teen years seemed to coincide with the parents' absence – the incident when I accidentally thrust a garden fork through Geraldine's hand a week before her final piano exams, the car accident with Gregory and the javelin to Jasmine William's stomach.

The launch of Queen Mary took place at about 11:00 a.m. The launch was from the dock of the culvert over the driveway, but Mary, with much recent misapprehension, refused to take to sea. After much cajoling and negative encouragement she was convinced to board. The first run was incident free, though there was a decided tendency of the keel-less vessel to rock. We walked her down the waterway, Steve on the left bank, Chris on the right, while I walked in the water at the stern. She sat stiffly in the bottom of the drum, tight-lipped, legs outstretched and white-knuckled where her little hands grasped the gunwale.

The second trip was also uneventful, with about another knot of speed added to test the lateral stability. Perhaps we could widen the ditch further and create a drag-pool using two boats. Perhaps this could become an Olympic event….

The third test was to determine the speed needed for the boat to hydroplane. By this time Mary was scared to death and screaming at the top of her lungs, much to everyone's amusement. A true test of hydroplaning required that the boat be vigorously pushed and then let go. We all pushed and let go. Out of our reach, Mary decided to jump ship, but as she stood, the absence of a keel became apparent. This was not computed into the design, since none of us had figured that we needed one. In a desperate attempt to get to dry land, Mary stepped on the gunwale, the boat turned turtle and she went down like a rock.

Hilarity arose among the gang, until Mary surfaced in a circle of bloody water. The sharp edge of the barrel had almost severed her big toe and it was all a muddy mess.

The natural urge of early teens faced with this circumstance was to bolt, as I had done a year or so earlier when I plunged the garden fork through Geraldine's hand, but the calm of Dawne prevailed and we lifted the wounded to triage on the front step. The wound was cleaned as we closed ranks and recited the story we had to tell to the parents.

There is no moral or lesson to be learnt from this episode, at least not for the perpetrators. Mary was whisked off to the doctor to have her toe stitched. Uncle Will had by then arrived to take Dawne and Steve back home and Chris and I were left to bear the terrible consequences of our parents' absence while the children were playing. As it turned out our clever stories and Chris' eloquent rendition of the events were unnecessary. Parents who give kids space expect them to occasionally (in our case often) screw up, and we had a lot of space growing up.

The day we burned the mountain
Sundays were truly a day of rest on the otherwise busy Browndale Farm. Church was at 7:00 a.m. at tiny St. Joseph's in Spanish Town followed by breakfast and then a morning at the beach. By 1957, Grandma Kelly had given up her house on Roosevelt Avenue and dedicated herself to travelling between her eleven children, who were by now scattered across North America, Jamaica and Britain. This meant that the weekly trek to Kingston ended and the family could settle into a more relaxed weekend, much of which was focused on the beach and exploring the Hellshire Hills.

The usual routine was a trip to Port Henderson, though every once in a while dad would head to Green Bay, just to add some variety. We would often stop on the way at Phoenix Park, one of the large farms that made up United Fruit Company's Bernard Lodge Estate, to pick up teenaged friends, Joan and Francis Brice. Keith Brice was the farm manager for Phoenix and he and wife Clitie were friends of our parents with whom we would often exchange visits. I then had a passing interest in Joan so these beach trips were a treat for me.

Port Henderson was directly across Kingston Harbour from Port Royal, and for the centuries that Spanish Town was the island capital, it was the main port for ships arriving in the island. It sat on a beach that ran from Fort Augusta to the north for two or so miles to the foot of Rodney's Lookout, known also as Port Henderson Hill, to the south. The road to the beach in 1960 petered out at the village, about a half mile from Port Henderson crossroads, and one had to drive around and across the sand dunes for another mile to reach the best beaches, near Fort Augusta. The sand dunes were up to ten feet tall in that area and were mostly covered in large sea grape trees. Further back from the narrow beach and dunes was a vast mangrove swamp which surrounded a lagoon known as Dawkins Pond, a crocodile infested but popular duck-hunting area in those days.

Green Bay Beach was tucked into a cove of Port Henderson Hill and was in an arid area. The beach was about a half mile long and was backed by a salt flat that ran to a steep hillside covered in cactus and thorny bush. This area was used by the army as a shooting range for mortars and light artillery and much of the area backing onto the hill was blocked off by concertina wire. A few hundred years earlier it had served as the cemetery for Port Royal following the earthquake of 1692, and in 1740 it became the site for Fort Clarence, built to defend the southern approaches to Spanish Town through the Great Salt Pond. Fort Clarence was a warren of concrete and brick structures that had been upgraded during World War II and renamed Fort Small. It was a great area to explore, with abandoned mortars, dozens of intact old buildings and even a paved water catchment area on the hillside that directed the meager rainfall into a huge tank. Some of the concrete structures on the salt flat that backed up to the beach still had a few broken up buildings that were used by the soldiers as target practice.

Being just outside the entrance to the harbour, one could often count on seeing sharks, so a lookout was in order whenever we were in the water. Reaching Green Bay meant a rough ride over a broken stone road that was always in poor shape and often furrowed by the runoff from rainstorms. The road followed the contour of the hill and the entrance to the beach was a steeply plunging dirt road that most cars could not handle with a full load.

On this particular day, dad decided to have a group picnic at Green Bay, so we headed off, past the lazaretto and over the hill to the road down to the beach. The DuQuesnay and Brice families would meet us at the beach. It was just after Christmas so Stephen, Chris and I had an ample supply of firecrackers that were to be exploded that day. When we had to get out and walk the steep road to the beach, we were looking for things to blow up. Our main weapon was the Thunderbolt. It was about four inches long and about half-inch wide and was capable of blowing off a finger. We saw a large branching cactus plant and decided to see what a Thunderbolt would do to it. One was screwed into a hole in the body of the plant and set off as we hid behind a large rock. After the blast shattered the cactus, we ran down to the beach to cool off from the hot descent.

The DuQuesnay and Brice families soon arrived and a group of us set off to walk to the far end of the beach to explore Fort Clarence. On the way back, Steve pointed to the hill where a wisp of smoke was being whipped about by the strong trade winds that were a constant daily companion. "Paul, I think we are in trouble!" modulating the last word to emphasize his concern as we hurried back to the picnic site. By this time, dad was waiting on us and ordered us back up the hill to put out the fire. It was a hot, dry climb to the site of our folly and by the time I got there with Steve, it was a wall of flame. The grasses at this time of year were tinder dry and pushed by a thirty knot wind the fire was making quick progress up the hill. All we could do was to beat the flames with branches broken from the shrubs and throw the sandy soil on the embers using our bare hands. The road was a good fire line and soon Desmond DuQuesnay climbed up to help us. He was the only one that came to our assistance – dad made sure that for our irresponsible behaviour we were left to find a way to deal with the fire.

After about an hour we had beaten the flames down and the next hour was spent dousing the embers with sand. The burn was about twenty feet square and had we not put it out, it would have burnt the entire mountain and possibly blown into the cane fields of Bernard Lodge Estate. It was a close run thing and we learnt a hard lesson that day as we dragged our weary bodies back down the hill after missing lunch and all the beach activities we had looked forward to.

Chapter twelve

Plane Crash!

M om called to us from the back door of our house "Paul, Chris, I just got back from Spanish Town Hospital. There is a Colombian woman there who was in a plane crash last night at Port Henderson. She was the only survivor and she speaks no English. Her body is covered with hundreds of cactus prickles, which the nurses were pulling out with tweezers when I left. Matron called me after the Americans dropped her off by helicopter." So began the strange odyssey of Senorita Mendez.

In July of 1961 a vintage WWII DC3 in the service of a Colombian freight company flew into Port Henderson Hill. En route from Barranquilla to Miami and loaded with garments that had been sewn for export to the USA, the old plane had landed to refuel at Palisadoes Airport the previous evening. Taking off later that night and groaning under the load, it was not able to climb the seven hundred feet needed to clear the hill six miles from the end of the runway.

Early the next morning we set off on our bicycles on the ride to Port Henderson, picking up Ronnie DuQuesnay along the way. The ride was a pleasant one through the rolling sugar cane fields of the United Fruit Company's Bernard Lodge estate. After nine miles we came up on the quiet country corner of Naggo's Head, named after the severed head of a slave of an earlier era, stopping for a drink at the only shop there. The last mile was down a marl road to the sea then a steep ride around the flank of Port Henderson Hill. This was an area well know to us. It was close to Port Henderson Beach, where we spent many Sundays after church. It was close to Green Bay which we boys had explored thoroughly on crab-hunting trips over the years and to the Great Salt Pond, which separated Port Henderson Hill from the rest of the arid Hellshire Hills.

We hid our bikes in the bushes near the Lazaretto and took the path to the right leading to Rodney's Lookout on the crest of the hill. The area is reminiscent of the Arizona Desert, bare rock covered with tall cactus and thorny scrubs, and it is one of the driest areas in Jamaica. The mile-long path was somewhat overgrown and obviously little-used since Admiral Rodney had used it to track the French Navy in Napoleonic times. It was a hot climb, and after about twenty minutes we rounded a corner to the sight of a swath of levelled vegetation just short of the stone tower of the lookout. The DC3 had approached from the direction of the airport to the east and had simply flown into the hill about seventy feet from the crest. We turned off the path into this clearing and followed it up to the crest of the ridge, a distance of about a hundred feet. The plane hit and then slid up the slope, shedding its port wing halfway up as it hit a rock, spinning the fuselage to the left. This was where Sra Mendez was ejected, still in her seat, through the gap in the fuselage and flung headlong into a large clump of organ-pipe cactus. Ironically, it was the cactus that cushioned her and saved her life. As the wingless fuselage crested the hill, now sliding sideways, it fell over a fifty-foot cliff, killing the two pilots. The slide area was littered with airplane parts and empty fire extinguishers.

Looking out from this hill top was a virtual history lesson covering five centuries. To the northwest lay Spanish Town, founded by the first Spaniards to settle in Jamaica in 1504. Port Royal, the British naval base and home to Captain Morgan, the famous pirate lay below us to the east, a third of its size after the 1692 earthquake submerged most of the town. Fort Agusta stood a couple of miles to the north, one of eleven forts guarding the approach to Spanish Town and mentioned by Lady Nugent, the 1804 Governor's wife. The US Aircraft carrier represented the future of this nation as the British withdrew to their homeland under pressure of the Americans to end colonialism. The runway from which the doomed airplane departed was clearly visible to the east. The carrier USS Lake Champlain was still peacefully at anchor in the harbour closer to Kingston and it was from there that rescue helicopters were launched. This must have been a difficult night landing on the clearing on the slope. The Americans had immediately taken the lady, still strapped into her seat, to the open grounds of Spanish Town Hospital. We collected some souvenirs and hiked the track back to our bikes and then wearily rode home.

The lady had no broken bones but was horribly mangled. Unable to speak any English in a town where few spoke Spanish, she remained in hospital for a week and was then flown back to Colombia. She was a supervisor at the air freight company and had hitched a ride on the freight flight to Miami. It was almost her last.

Chapter thirteen

Train Journeys

J amaica was blessed with a well-organized railway service, with over two hundred miles of track and in my teen years I made some memorable journeys by train. The first time I rode the train was in 1960 from Spanish Town to Kingston on the way to cadet camp. This trip was just ten miles through the cane fields of St. Catherine to a siding at Gregory Park and then through the Caymanas swamps to Kingston. At that time, the passenger cars were attached to a regular freight train pulled by a single coal powered steam engine. My recollection of that first trip was a great clatter and jostling of the cars and a top speed of about forty miles per hour. The station in Kingston was an elegant cast iron structure that dated back to when the first rails were laid in the mid-1840s and though it was in good repair, it was in a seedy part of town, right next to the docks and the slaughter house and not far from the slum called 'Back-a-wall'.

The next trip was in 1963 to Port Antonio. The cadet camp that year was held at the Boundbrook School and I foolishly volunteered to be a part of the set up crew – the labour force for setting up the camp. The British Army was still a presence in Jamaica and lorries took us to the supply area at the main army camp in Kingston where we requisitioned and loaded all the supplies onto the trucks. The next stop was the train station in Kingston where we loaded the supplies onto boxcars and the next morning we set off for Port Antonio.

This line branched from the Montego Bay line at Spanish Town and headed north through Bog Walk Gorge to Linstead then branched again from the Ewarton line and looped through St. Mary, turning east and hugging the coast, finally entering Port Antonio from the west. The stops along the way were as exotic as they were interesting. The line from Spanish Town ran for a few miles and then passed the Angels siding. There was nothing to distinguish Angels except that this was where one of the few industrial plants in Jamaica stood, the Ariguanabo Textile Mill with its four hundred workers and a siding to load cloth and unload cotton. The line then climbed into the rugged limestone foothills through which the Rio Cobre gorge was cut, entering a mile-long tunnel as it cut through the hard white rock of the highest part of the gorge. This was one of the longest railway tunnels in the world when it was blasted out with gunpowder in the 1850s, and because of its length the conductors made everyone close the carriage windows to keep the coal smoke out. The walls of the tunnel were stained with the soot of over one hundred years of coal-burning trains. Just when it looked like the tunnel would never end, we popped out onto a steep stone wall high above the river. We then went clanging across an old iron bridge and slowed to a stop with a billowing cloud of steam at the Bog Walk station. The fruit vendors swarmed the train, as in every third world country with a train system, selling tangerines, oranges, jackfruit, coconuts and sweetsops.

After a wait of a few minutes for the market vendors and students to detrain, a loud whistle and the jostling of the wooden passenger cars signaled that we were on our way again. We shifted to the Port Antonio line as the train approached the Bybrook sugar factory. The lurching that signaled the switch to the new line soon stopped and we chugged along to Riversdale where we again stopped at a siding where bananas were loaded onto a boxcar. My dad operated a banana farm in Riversdale back in 1938 and I wondered if some of the fruit being loaded came from that same farm. We were soon off again, and after a series of short tunnels, we rolled into Troja on the St. Mary parish line. Troja sat in a verdant valley surrounded by rolling hills that were all covered in coconut, banana and cocoa trees. Again the stop was to load bananas destined for the United Fruit Company wharf in Port Antonio.

A few miles further along we passed the Richmond Prison farm, stopping at a siding amidst the well-tended fields of banana and citrus. This facility was for white-collar criminals and housed fallen middle class Jamaicans who had been convicted of fraud and other non-violent crimes. The prisoners were all serving sentences at hard labour and could be seen in their white shorts and shirts working in the fields. Beyond Richmond, the line twisted and turned through tunnels and embankments in the hills of St. Mary and suddenly exited onto the wide banks of the Wag Water River. For economical reasons, the railway line shared this and other bridges on the remainder of the journey with the North Coast highway and as we approached, the gate tender would run out and close the gate, blocking road traffic. It was curious, but this and all the other bridges and level crossings each had a cottage where the gate tender lived with his family. There were no more than four trains per day along these tracks, so it must have been the ideal job for someone who didn't really want to work.

We soon passed the flatlands around the Gray's Inn sugar factory at Agualta Vale and slowed to a hissing stop at Annotto Bay. The sea was muddy as the Wag Water River was in spate and the sky was overcast as we eased out of the station into a rainstorm. The imposing Great House was just visible through the rain, sitting proudly on the hill at Iter Boreale as we chugged by at the top speed for the line of about 40 mph. The next stop was the ornate cut-stone station at Buff Bay, which sat on the banks of a stagnant river, surrounded by stately Royal palms and otaheiti apple trees. Otaheiti apples were introduced from Tahiti by Captain Bligh and at that time of year they covered the ground beneath them with a blanket of vivid violet blossoms. The area was obviously rainier than most, judging from the mass of epiphytes growing on the tree trunks. Buff Bay was the market town for the high mountain valleys and the banana loading took a full half-hour, with each bunch brought into a boxcar on the head of a porter. The boxcar was lined with banana leaf trash, which acted as packing to reduce bruising of the fruit. I wondered why the buying station simply did not have a car left in a siding so that it could be loaded before the train got there.

The bay was flat calm as the rain eased and we chugged out of the station along the black sand beach, past the extinct volcano at Black Hill. This was the only volcano in Jamaica but only a geologist could tell because it had no cone and looked just like the other hills in the area. The line soon slithered down to the beach, continuing along it for the next few miles. Even though the line would get washed away with each passing hurricane, this was probably the best place to put the line because the hills reached down to the sea. Along this stretch, there were dozens of women sitting astride piles of gravel that they had pounded out of the hard black volcanic rock to make gravel for the rail bed. These women were paid by the cubic yard and it was one of the few jobs available in much of rural Jamaica. Tourists taking the train from Port Antonio at the turn of the century were known to write that they saw gangs of 'prisoners' breaking stones, as it must have seemed to them that only prisoners would do that sort of work!

The next stop was the station at Hope Bay, with another banana stop and soon we were speeding along past the coconut plantations at St. Margaret's Bay. The line ran close to an airstrip that had been hacked out of the coconut trees. A few years later, I used that airstrip for stops on cross-country flights for my pilot's license. The railway line ran over the Rio Grande iron bridge and past the Rafter's Rest at the mouth of the river. Rafter's Rest was the final stop for the bamboo rafts that plied the river from Berrydale, loaded with tourists. Soon after, we rounded the bluff to the east of Port Antonio and slid into the terminus at Boundbrook. It must have rained ten times during the journey with heavy, short downpours between Buff Bay and Port

Antonio and we got off the train in the eleventh downpour. This did not stop the unloading, though; Port Antonio got over two hundred inches of rain and work had to continue. The banana boat was at the wharf next to the station and hundreds of porters descended on the train to unload the bananas directly to the boat. The set up platoon, numbering about twenty five cadets, walked across the road to Boundbrook School which was our destination for a week of cadet camp.

The following year, I travelled from Spanish Town to Montego Bay on what was to become an annual pilgrimage to Montego Bay Yacht Week at Easter. By this time, the railway had replaced the original passenger cars with diesel powered two-car carriages. Train travel was a lot more pleasant without the blowing soot that was a feature of steam train travel.

This was a journey through some of the most interesting countryside, most of which was not accessible by road. Pulling out of Spanish Town station, we moved slowly for the first mile or so, past the spot where Dessie DuQuesnay had shot a man a couple of years before in an incident that that was to divide the town. Dessie was seventeen at the time and was patrolling his father's farm when he encountered a group of youths running from a field. He claimed that he tried to shoot over their heads with the shotgun but did not expect that the scatter pattern would be so wide. While in jail, for his own safety, he was held on the death row wing of the Spanish Town prison. His cellmate was the notorious revolutionary Reynold Henry, who had led an uprising in July 1960 in which two British soldiers were executed. This was a curious pairing of prisoners, since Henry was an established white-hating revolutionary who was seeking a Rastafarian-run, Cuban-backed government, but they struck up a friendship and Dessie was to witness Henry being taken from the cell on the day he was executed. Dessie got off the murder charge and then had to leave the country to avoid retribution.

The track was elevated a few feet above the windblown cane fields and ran for a straight stretch of about seven miles through Innswood Estate. A few months later on this very stretch, during a flying lesson,

Bobby Dixon my flight instructor, in a fit of spontaneity, 'shot up' a steam train. We were merrily flying along on a check flight when we spotted a train. He looked at me with an impish smile and peeled off in a split-s as he must have done flying in the RAF in the war, getting down almost level with the cane tops and flying over the tracks towards the train. About a half mile away and closing fast, we spotted a brakeman standing on top of a car and Bobbie's grin widened as he firewalled the throttle. The poor brakeman spotted us a few seconds later and started running furiously to the back of the train, hopping the gap from one car to the next. Bobbie pulled up a few hundred yards from the engine and then, from a few feet above the train cars, rushed towards the brakeman. As we flew over him, he made a mad dive down the ladder between cars. Bobbie pulled up just short of the Heartlands siding, tears streaming down his face.

Back on the train, we soon flew through the Heartlands siding and headed to the first stop at Bushy Park. The hundred mile ride was to last five hours, because we stopped at every station and siding on the route, even if there were no passengers leaving or coming aboard. For the next hour or so, the 'Diesel' wound its way through the flat lands of St. Catherine and Clarendon, stopping at Old Harbour, Sandy Bay, Inverness, May Pen, Glenroy, and Clarendon Park, then it started up the steep incline to Porus. Porus was in the foothills of the Manchester mountains, one of the fruit capitals of the country, and the train was soon surrounded by vendors selling twenty or so different types of fruit.

The next few miles to Williamsfield, the stop for Mandeville, was one of the steepest sections of the line, moving up a steep slope on the Melrose Hill section. The air cooled as we climbed into Williamsfield and soon we were close to the Alcan Alumina refinery at Shooters Hill, smelling the acrid caustic soda used in alumina production and seeing the vast red mud lake where the refuse from the refinery was dumped. My dad had told us an interesting story about Shooters Hill. A rich man had made it known that when he died he wanted to be buried at the highest point in the region, but Shooters Hill was so steep that there was no road and the coffin had to be carried about five hundred feet by hand up to the crest. Shooters Hill was also the location of the Pickapeppa factory; the owner, a Mr. Joseph Lynn Kee Chow bought the rights from Norman Nash in 1921 to the world-famous sauce that Nash had concocted in his kitchen from a blend of spices. Joseph was supposed to be the only person who knew the formulation of the sauce, which was kept in a bank vault, much like the Coca-Cola formula.

Kendal was the next stop; that was a name burnt into the consciousness of all Jamaicans who had memories of that tragic day in 1957 when a passenger train had crashed, killing 184 people. The wheel bogies could still be seen, sitting in the weeds off to the side of the cutting where the train derailed, probably at the crest of the line.

The mountains closed in and surrounded us as we slowly passed through the next stations at Grove Place, Mile Gully, Balaclava and Siloah, then we descended to the valley floor where we passed the spectacular setting of Appleton Estate. Appleton sat in the Black River valley and was a flat-bottomed valley that suddenly appeared, completely surrounded by hills. Some of the finest sugar cane in the island grew there and its rum refinery was world-renowned.

The track continued on, following the river valley to Maggotty. Maggotty was an important stop on this line as it served the maroon town at Accompong and was the site of the famous Black River Falls. The next fifteen miles of the track skirted the wondrous Cockpit Country. The many conical hills rose sharply above the valley floors; their slopes were almost vertical and covered with dense jungle. Few roads penetrated this region and the track was a marvel of nineteenth century construction. The track bed was literally hacked from the hills with numerous tunnels and sharp curves. The vines hung hundreds of feet from the hills above the track, adding to the mystery of the place. It was in these hills that two centuries earlier the Maroons (escaped slaves) fought the British Army to a standstill and forced the British to concede to them a self-governing reservation.

The exquisitely pretty villages of Ipswich and Stonehenge were the next two stops and a blond, blue eyed family got off. We speculated that they were part of the German community that had moved to

Seaford Town in the 1830s, and were surprised that they had managed to keep Germanic features after a century's stirring of the melting pot. At Catadupa, we stopped and pulled off on a siding to let the 'Governor's Coach' pass. This was a tourist train that stopped at Appleton and was very popular up until it was cancelled a decade later. The next stop was Cambridge, then Seven Rivers, then Montpelier in the verdant valley of the Great River. Two miles down the track, we stopped at Mount Carey then Anchovy. Montego Bay came into view as we descended to the cane fields of Barnett Estate and soon we sided to a stop at the terminus on the south side of Montego Bay.

After its start in 1845 with tracks from Kingston to Spanish Town, the rails were extended to Port Antonio and Montego Bay, with spurs Ewarton and Chapleton added by 1897. By this time there were over two hundred miles of track, but the succession of companies that owned the company were never profitable. The expansion of the road system started the decline of the railway. The train service ended in stages starting in the mid 1970s when banana shipping was moved from Port Antonio. That line was completely abandoned in 1980 when Hurricane Allen's huge waves destroyed the coast-hugging line from Buff Bay to Port Antonio. The passenger traffic was ended in the early 1980s, and soon after the popular Governor's Coach service was shut down. Today only the alumina freight service remains. One can feel the absence of these magnificent machines that started with such promise in the 1840s. There are reports that the Chinese Government is helping rehabilitate the track in 2008 and one wonders if the right of way has succumbed to squatters during the hiatus of service.

My train journeys, over the short period of a decade spanned the entire period of propulsion, starting with the sooty, chugging and hissing coal-fuelled steam trains with engines named 'Engine 54', to the street-car-like, self propelled passenger cars, to the huge, chest throbbing diesel-electric engines that have more recently been used to haul alumina and freight. If for no other reason, I hope that the train service in Jamaica is restored so that one can again enjoy passing through the interior of this glorious island with all the wonderfully named towns. Catadupa, Siloah, Maggotty, Anchovy – where else can one find adopted names that roll off the tongue with such fluency?

Chapter fourteen

The Independence Caper

J amaica had been an English colony since 1655. It was wrested from the Spanish as an afterthought after General Penn's taskforce failed in its bid to capture Haiti, then the most valuable property in the hemisphere. After a failed attempt to combine all the English-speaking islands of the Caribbean into a federation and under pressure from the USA, England decided to give independence to Jamaica in mid-1962. Jamaica refused to take Cayman and the Turks & Caicos Islands as they were too poor and would have been a drag on the treasury.

With all the pomp and circumstance then available, the island prepared for the great day on August 6, 1962 when the Union Jack would be lowered and the new Jamaican flag raised. Jamaica would soon be free of the British teachers, who made life difficult by requiring discipline and an attempt at learning. We would have control of our government and we would run our little country quite well, thank you. A new sports stadium was being readied and it did not seem that it would be built in time, so a large part of the former British Army campground was taken to site the stadium. Perhaps this was a symbol of the times.

The celebrations were unforgettable, with a member of the Royal family lowering the Union Jack while the new Prime Minister raised the new Jamaican flag. The best fireworks of the century were to follow. Chris, Ronnie DuQuesnay, Dawne and I garnered parental approval to attend, and the 18-year old Ronnie with his newly minted driver's permit would drive. His mother's 1956 model Austin A60 was pressed into service and a route was researched and committed to memory.

We left Spanish Town at about 5:00 p.m., and after endless traffic delays managed to stick the car into a tiny parking spot on the road to Beverly Hills. Clambering through the brush, we walked up the slope and found an overlook that looked down on the National Stadium. Even from over a mile away the music and the cheering were evident and the preliminaries dragged on for about three hours. The fireworks started at about 9:00 p.m. and lasted for about 2 hours. They were spectacular, especially since none of us had seen much more that the odd backyard bottle-rocket. As things wound down, we started our homeward trek. Kingston was eleven miles from Spanish Town – much too far a journey for thirsty youngsters and we stopped off at the Rainbow Drive Inn for cokes and a patty. Time was running out on our curfew, so we decide to eat in the car.

The Washington Boulevard was the newer of the two highways that led west, and we took it. At that time it had just been built and there were few houses along it. As we approached the Molynes Road junction, Ronnie pulled over onto the shoulder, and while still moving at about forty mph, we tossed the empty bottles into the bushes. Just as we started heading back onto the road, we caught sight of a drunk who had been standing on the edge of the pavement, attempting to cross the street. He staggered back in our direction in a failed attempt to escape, and a few seconds later, to our horror, he was lying in the middle of the intersection. Hitting him had taken out the windshield and the right side mirror and he had put huge dents in the hood and top when he rolled off the top, onto the hood. As soon as he hit the ground, we started rehearsing our story. A passing motorist saw the incident and told us to take the man to hospital since there was a need for medical attention for this obviously unconscious person. This gave us a reason to leave the scene of an accident, and would make it impossible for the police to see that we were off the road at the point of contact. This sounded good, so we bundled him into the back seat and headed off to the University hospital.

There were two problems. We had insufficient gas to get home and we had no money to buy gas. Between the four of us, we were able to find eight pence, enough to buy about two quarts, but we were not sure about waking a gas station attendant and asking for a half gallon of gas; this would not be viewed with humour at 1:30 a.m. Dawne got drafted to do the evil deed. She woke the attendant by banging on the glass and telling him to pump until she told him when to stop. When the meter clicked over to a half-gallon she shouted for him to stop, we dropped the money on the ground and sped off, with a withering cascade of cuss words following us.

Splinters showered us all in the front seat as Ronnie drove, so we knocked out the remaining glass and continued practising our story. We were to learn later that the man was drunk but conscious all this time and listening to this feeble plotting. This was to cost Ronnie's father.

A young Trinidadian intern took care of the man, and after a half-hour or so of nervous waiting he announced to Ronnie that the man was ok, with just a small cut on the hand and a mild concussion. Apparently the white rum had served him well by making him limp for the blow. This was to become one of the incidents that steered Ronnie and Chris into medicine, or so they told us a few years later. It is rumoured that it cost Mr. DuQuesnay a couple hundred pounds to hush the man.

We reached home at about 3:00 a.m. to a hellishly worried Mom and Mr. DuQuesnay, who had driven around to see if my parents knew what had caused the delay. This is the sort of incident with which children burden parents, and the cycle continues as our children who do stupid things through bombast and inexperience have also burdened us. The cycle of life goes on.

Chapter fifteen

Hurricane!

I t takes a traumatic event to imprint lasting memories on a young mind and the great Hurricane Charlie of 1951 was such an event. During my childhood, Jamaica was somewhat fortunate as it lay just south of the main Atlantic hurricane track and it was only every decade or so that the country would get as much as a rain shower from a hurricane, and thirty or so years between direct hits. Charlie hit Jamaica directly and catastrophically.

The house at Browndale had just been expanded the previous year for the birth of Mary, my youngest sister, and it was this new room that provided the only place of refuge at the height of the storm. Unlike the rest of the house, the 'New Room' was of sturdy reinforced concrete construction and although it shared a zinc roof with the rest of the building, it proved to be well built and held on to be the only undamaged part of the house. It was to be our shelter for the three months that reconstruction lasted.

The day of the hurricane started calm and sultry with a brilliant sunset giving no hint of what was to come. We had heard the radio reports from earlier in the week but the forecasting in those days was at best imprecise, so other than our parents not too many people in the area paid much attention. Dad boarded up the windows as best he could and we settled in as though it was a normal night.

At about midnight, I awoke to the indescribable howling of the wind and felt the steady drip of water on my face. I scurried out to my parent's room to the scornful ridicule of Chris. "You little coward! Mama's boy! Mama's boy!" Chris and I shared the windowless middle room in the house and it would have seemed that if that room went then the whole house would go. After another half-hour of the most furious battering, mom and dad evacuated their bedroom and we all ended up in the new room, except for seven-year old Chris who, even then, would laugh in the face of adversity.

We could hear and feel every shudder as sections of the roof departed or as some large object slammed into the house, and then at about three in the morning there was a tremendous swoosh followed by screams from Chris. Dad felt his way through the darkness to find Chris on a collapsed bed, pounded into the floor by the collapsed ceiling. The room was about 15 feet square, and apparently after the roof blew off, the ceiling had remained in place collecting hundreds of gallons of water, eventually collapsing onto the sleeping Chris. Fortunately it had hinged on one side and opened in trapdoor fashion, dumping water but no lumber. Not so brave now, he was brought shivering and whimpering to the new room.

The storm shrieked through the night and the morning dawned bleak and gray, with steady rain. As the light returned and the rain slowed, my lasting impression was of a moonscape. There were few trees left standing, and those that remained upright were bereft of limbs and leaves. There was only brown and grey, not a leaf remained on a tree. The huge guango trees were toppled, leaning crazily or broken and the few coconut trees that survived had their nuts strewn about. Our front yard was covered by two feet of water, as was everywhere else. You could almost see Spanish Town, some three miles to the east.

At about noon dad was able to get out and check on the cattle. Well-disciplined and perhaps waiting to be milked, the entire herd had stayed in the demolished holding pen. The roof of the house was 75% gone, as was a large part of the rafters. The mesh that covered the windows and lattice verandah was largely gone. There was already the smell of decay that was to stay with us for the next three months.

Relief from the storm came quickly, with the government handing out clothes that had been collected in Britain, Canada and the USA. The parish council office in each parish was the drop off point, with the Secretary of the Council responsible for distributing to local districts. The Secretary in the British system was the equivalent of the parish manager and wielded great clout. It was not unknown for these gentlemen to take advantage of these types of situations, selling rather than giving relief goods to people. My dad was relentless and ended up cussing out our parish council and ended up being appointed the distribution point for central St. Catherine. Soon there were mounds of second hand clothes heaped on our lawn with a seemingly endless stream of people, mostly women from the area, picking through the winter coats, prom dresses and other inappropriate apparel that had been graciously donated by our northern neighbours.

Slowly, piles of zinc sheets with dad's initials painted on the underside identifying them as part of our roof, were returned from outlying districts. Uncle John Vasina arrived by car a few days later from Kingston to check if we survived and shot a whole reel of 8mm colour film showing the devastation on the way and at our farm. The film, viewed four decades later showed dad walking out of the remains of the house with pipe in mouth, showed the broken roof and the litter of five young Virtue children playing in the pond that had covered our front yard.

Within three weeks, another hurricane was reported to be heading straight for Jamaica, and as we listened to the hourly radio reports on the Grundig Radio, the situation seemed grim. The roof was not fully on and electricity had just returned. The Catholics of the country organized a prayer vigil at the eastern end of the island and perhaps in response to their prayers, the storm took a ninety-degree turn to the north and completely missed the island, after approaching within a hundred miles. They continue this to this day, over a half-century later. Since then, and up until 2005, only Hurricane Gilbert in 1988 has hit the island directly, though in the first decade of the century hurricanes have again become more frequent and each year Jamaica has seen a large number of storms come close enough to cause major flood and wind damage.

Chapter sixteen

Christopher's Car

The Ford Anglia (the flying car from the Harry Potter movie), built for the masses, was a study in British minimalism. It sat on a sturdy chassis with a 900cc engine and cranked out a mighty 50 horsepower. It had a rakish back windshield that was angled inward at the bottom, the semblance of tail fins and browed headlights. Christopher's Anglia was bright lime green, a 1959 model, right-hand drive with a stick-shift. This was his 'wheels' in the mid-1960s while at the University of the West Indies. He abused this car. He loved this car. Neglect, the child of student poverty was the most obvious emotion of this troubled relationship.

I recall driving the same car to the beach at about age 17 so this was one of the family's cars from about 1963 and had been paired with the Ferguson farm tractor as the training vehicle for the boys. The reason for our parent's generosity is lost to memory. Perhaps in a moment of weakness our parents decided to overlook Chris' dedication to daring, craziness and just plain fun.

He took this car on campus in 1964 and commenced to wreak havoc. The first incident involved engine oil. The little dashboard lights were some of the few instruments working and the red one next to the little oil can symbol must have been suggesting something since it had been on for a few days. Perhaps it was time to check it out. One of Chris' buddies suggested engine ruination but Chris had no money for oil. I was the closest person that might have money and at the time was probably hanging out at our cousin Anthony's house about four miles away. The problem was that I was an avid Saturday afternoon matinee moviegoer so when Chris arrived unannounced for oil money, I was at the Carib movie theatre with my arm around a young lady. Disappointed but not defeated, Chris then set off for cousin Steve's house for the oil loan. A half-mile down the road, the main crankshaft bearings revolted and the blacksmith started hammering in the crankcase. Still not accepting defeat, Chris coasted into a gas station, hit up the manager for three quarts of oil, and rocked the car back and forth with the optimistic expectation of unseizing the engine. The car was towed away for an engine rebuild, much to dad's chagrin.

The second incident was a run in with a Jamaica Omnibus Service city bus. Chris swore that the stop sign was missing on his side of the intersection and survived on the skill of the bus driver, crushing the driver-side door and taking out a grove of roadside coolie plum trees. There was no money to fix the broken door lock and it was too soon to again face the wrath of dad, so Chris resorted to Boy Scout inventiveness. He strapped the door to the door pillar with about ten wraps of number fourteen electrical wire, found on the roadside. The car remained in this condition even as the battery died for a lack of water. The battery and the door posed no particular challenge except when starting the engine. He always made sure he parked on a slope so he could easily kick-start it by releasing the hand brake and gaining a rolling start. The combination of damaged door and dead battery was to wreak destruction on the offending omnibus line a few months later.

Chris had been dating a professor's daughter who lived about a mile from campus. Hope Boulevard was a steep, wide road, ideal for kick starting, so he had no premonition of disaster when he pulled up to the curb that night to pick up his date. The electrical wire binding the door on the driver's side meant he had to get in through the passenger door, squeezing over the hand brake and shoe-horning into the right hand seat. The problem this time was that he had parked too close to the curb and it would not budge when he released the brake. After swearing silently, he figured that his best bet was to have his date steer while he pushed. Unfortunately, the girl had never driven a car, but no problem. After a lesson in the theory of kick starting, he helped her into the driver's seat but the girl panicked and would not do it. Chris' next best plan was for him to do both pushing and driving, a gymnastic feat when the driver's door does not work. His brilliant strategy was to push from the left hand side and, as the car started its roll, grab open the left hand door, leap in, jump over the passenger seat, squeeze across the transmission hump and handbrake, then stick it in first gear, turn the ignition on and release the clutch. The fact that he really thought this was possible is a testament to his optimism.

The car gathered speed at the gentlest of urging, getting away from him as he tripped over the curb. He was now in flat out pursuit of his car, cussing loudly. The car beat him to the junction with Old Hope Road, ran a red light and ended up taking out the Mona Heights bus shed. Luckily the bus shed was built of less sturdy stuff, and the car did not sustain any more damage. After extricating shed from car with the help of a group of passing boys, Chris was still able to go on his date.

Well-bred local girls all seemed to believe in eternal virginity. This led many hormone-crazed, young men of mid-sixties Jamaica to try their luck with tourist girls. The story that was spread by those who had a reputation as players was that American girls were easy, and those of us who aspired to be players had no trouble believing the rumours. Chris as usual had no money, but possessed the hormones and the car. Hanging out with a younger brother was just not cool, but I had some money. This was the perfect symbiotic relationship which set the stage for a very interesting, incident-filled weekend at Cousin Kenny's house in Oracabessa. Although I had no driver's license I insisted that I drive, telling Chris that I needed to practice for my license test. In truth, my brother's driving scared the crap out of me and I trusted my shaky skills over his on the winding Junction Road that led north out of Kingston up the Wag Water River valley. Strength of cash prevailed and sealed the deal. I would drive.

We set off this Friday afternoon on our two hour, sixty mile odyssey and after no more than ten miles, Chris was fussing that I was driving "like a snail" and that we would arrive at the Tower Isle Hotel too late for the best pickings. Using force of personality, interspersed with threats and a few dozen cuss words, he finally convinced me that it was in everybody's interest that he do the driving. Thirty minutes later, he found that a motor scooter driver was also driving too slowly and overtook him on a blind corner, cutting him off to avoid an onrushing country bus and almost depositing this unfortunate soul over a five hundred foot cliff into the Wag Water River. Somehow the scooter rider survived as the Anglia sped off.

Justice was done, however. Ten miles up the road, at Agualta Vale, the left rear tire blew out under the stress of two-wheel cornering. Chris got out and instead of doing something useful, started swearing and kicking the car. "What the hell is your problem, Chris?" I yelled. "I sold the jack to buy gas!" Chris shouted back. A hastily drawn plan was concocted to complete the tire change before the irate scooter rider arrived. I was to lift the car while he slipped off the flat tyre and replaced it with the spare. All 127 pounds of me strained to lift the car and after two minutes, a slipped disc and fingers permanently crooked into a semi-closed claw, I gave up. The scooter rider rode up, dismounted with a cheery "Good evening, can I help?" and helped lift the car. He was either an idiot or a seminarian.

At this point, I refused to get back into the car unless I was driving. He again relented. There were no further incidents until just before we arrived at Tower Isle. It was starting to get dark and as I turned on the headlights, the warning light for the battery lit up. "Chris, we have a problem!" I said. "No problem. Stop over there", Chris replied, pointing to a low bank next to one of the ubiquitous dry-stacked stone walls found in the area. He popped the hood and climbed the bank, selecting the largest stone he could lift. "Damn, he is going to kill the car!" I thought, as he started pounding something inside the engine compartment. "What the hell are you doing?" I shouted. "...lost the generator tension bolt last month." he responded, as he pounded a portion of a tree trunk back into place in the engine. Apparently he had ingeniously wedged the tree as a tensioner between generator and engine block and it had worked itself loose.

Back on the road, we soon arrived at Kenny's house, which was just up the hill from the Tower Isle Hotel. Kenny was either a really trusting soul or he was just plain dumb, as he had left the house in Robin's charge. Robin was a cousin with a sweet gift of gab and robust charm, but at sixteen years old, absolutely no sense of responsibility. There were no end of parties at this house and by the end of the week, every single female tourist at the Tower Isle was convinced that Robin was a successful tycoon who had made his fortune in South American emeralds, that I was a fighter pilot and that Chris was a celebrity surgeon.

Chris turned out to be the smartest of the three, though; seeing no value in pursuing giddy American girls who were just as prudish as their Jamaican middle-class counterparts. He ran off with the roving entertainment troupe that put on the limbo show at the Tower Isle. Rumour placed him with the limbo dancer-girls at two other show venues that weekend.

These were the early days of the USA's involvement in Vietnam, and the first girls that Robin and I selected soaked up all of Cousin Kenny's liquor, made wonderful conversation but professed eternal love for their boyfriends who were Green Berets in Vietnam. For the love of country they would remain eternally faithful. It was not until a few years later that we realized that these girls were playing us equally. That was to be the theme for the week – charming conversations, a lot of rum but mission failure. No one knew for sure about Chris, though. He arrived back at Kenny's at 4:00 a.m. of the morning that we were due back in Kingston.

With a heavy knock on the front door, he announced his arrival and demanded that we leave within the next half-hour. He refused, on the basis that he was a man of honour and a gentleman, to say where he had been and what he had been doing for three days. He was obviously too tired to drive, so I took the helm for the long drive home.

The gas gauge was bouncing off the 'empty' stop, and fearing that the spare tire may have been sold in the missing three days to pay for gas, I asked no questions. The Ocho Rios gas station at the foot of Fern Gully was the closest that was open at 5:00 a.m. After coaxing the car for fifteen miles, we drew into the gas station. The park brake, called an 'emergency brakc' is an essential piece of equipment in hilly Jamaica and ranked up there with the battery, the jack and the spare tire. When I pulled into the gas station and yanked on the park brake, the handle came all the way up. The weird sound that had been coming from underneath the car all the way from Tower Isle must have been the broken cable skipping off the roadway.

Somehow we survived these youthful escapades more or less intact. Chris is now the famous doctor that he was destined to be, catering to the dermatological needs of Palm Beach socialites, though with the occasional Dr. Schweitzer-esque mission to the poor of the Cayman Islands. I almost became that famous fighter pilot, flying for a while until my eyes failed from the strain of too many late night quests for loose women. I was eventually rescued from my futile quest by Olivene, who married me before I could find any loose women. Robin, after many furious years of fun, found religion and settled down to a dignified life of tending emerald-coloured bushes as a landscape specialist on the west coast of Florida.

Chapter seventeen

Those Magnificent Men

"*D*on't let that bother you!" Victor Beek shouted cheerily over the urgent whooping of the stall warning claxon as I sat in the airplane's right seat contemplating eternity. A stall warning in the belly of a cloud still two thousand feet from the end of the runway is not a cheery sound. We were on approach to Boscobel Airfield in a new Jamaica Defence Force aircraft flown by an old Royal Air Force pilot who approached flying with the disdain of a pickpocket. Victor was just one of many pilots I would fly with in the mid 1960s whose survival of WWII seemed to imbue them – in their own minds – with a sense of indestructibility.

I had come to flying through the first pilot training program of the Army and Air Cadet Force and loved every minute of it. The training program was initially underwritten by ex-RAF officers who had returned to Jamaica from fighting in the war. Now successful businessmen and still dedicated to flying, they were the core of the local flying club. These men gave freely of their time, and their aircraft, to bring a new crop of pilots to the fore in a country where few could afford the cost of more formal overseas training. I was lucky to be one of four students selected for a flying scholarship in 1963 and received my license in early 1964. This was six months before I was old enough to sit a driving license test.

My first ever flight had been two years earlier, coincidentally with Victor Beek, my current instructor. As we rose above the ground and puttered along at all of seventy miles per hour, the neat quilt of the cane fields and the orderliness of the streets and rivers revealed themselves as no commercial flight ever could. The puffy clouds beckoned one to explore their dark valleys and brilliant white towers as they boiled upward, soon to be that afternoon's thunderstorms. Neat hamlets rolled by, surrounded by lush green forests all set against a background of shade and light where the slanting sunbeams played against mountain ridge and cloud. It was a joy to find a growing cloud and to circle it tightly with the lowered wingtip just brushing the seething mass. Victor made me take the controls that day and with simple instructions we were soon doing gentle turns with perfect coordination of rudder and aileron. Too soon we returned to earth in this wonder of a fabric-covered two-seater, possessing but one door, no flaps and a minimum of instruments.

Still in high school, I could not afford to rent an airplane but I would still take the bus or ride my bicycle and hang around the flying club or Wings Limited on weekends hoping that someone would take me up with them. Wings Limited was owned by Earsly and Carl Barnett and was a flying school where many Jamaican commercial pilots started their training. Earsly was almost totally deaf and it was amusing to fly with her and see how she faked hearing air traffic control instructions. The tower always knew from the flight plan that she had company that would relay their instructions, acknowledge, and thus spare her dignity. She was a black American who had built many flying hours ferrying B17 bombers from Boeing field in Seattle to England during the war and had considerably more hours in that type than nearly all the battle crews flying out of England. She was a magnificent pilot and the only one who would fly into some of the shorter hill strips in the island. Carl was a capable pilot but held down a full time job at the Carib Cement plant across the harbour and seldom participated in instruction. I would help gas up the planes and would share stories with students like John Sherlock who would later become chief pilot at British West Indian Airways. John was a stickler for rules and would chide me for showing up to fly too soon after a Saturday night party's worth of rum.

One thing I never relished was low flying and one Sunday morning we were put to the test by a newly minted pilot who was building hours on an aircraft type he had just been certified to fly. Freddie Ramson was middle-aged – unusual for a new pilot. He wanted to fly commercial light aircraft to ferry corporate executives around and maybe get a posting at the local airline, Trans Jamaica. Ian Roxburgh, a fellow student, came along for the ride that day as Freddie practiced his short field landings. The airplane was a low-wing type that the club had just purchased and had 'ground effect' handling characteristics a bit different from the high-wing types we typically flew. That nearly killed us that day. We took off with Freddie at the controls, Ian in the right seat and me in the back and headed across Kingston Harbour to Tinson Pen airstrip. Tinson Pen was being upgraded with a runway re-paving and the high-voltage power lines were being rerouted from the western approach. The first landing was high and fast to clear the cranes moving the power lines and after a few bounces and early dumping of flaps we just stopped at the runway end. This performance was repeated with a series of touch-and-go landings, and then we set off to an even shorter runway at Bernard Lodge Sugar Estate. That strip was a simple unpaved widening of a cart lane bordered by banana and cane fields. After one landing, Freddie was satisfied with his skills and we set off fast and low over the fields, heading towards the sea. We were so low that he had to pull up to get over the mangroves at the edge of the Great Salt Pond and then the small trees on the seashore. The next move was a tight left turn into Green Bay and this is what nearly put us into the water. The sea was shallow and crystal clear and in the early morning there was no wind to ripple the surface and render it visible. As we entered the turn I glanced out the window and saw the prop-wash furrowing the surface at no more than ten feet below us. He had misjudged his altitude and the wing blocking his view of the sea surface compounded this. A turn in a low wing airplane drops the inside wing of the turn a lot lower than in other airplanes and before I shouted for him to pull up, the left wing could not have been more than a few feet from the surface. He pulled up a bit and entered Green Bay at about thirty feet, immediately turning hard right to avoid flying into the hillside behind the bay. That was the last time I flew with Freddie. He went on to fly for 'Tinker' Rerrie at Jamaica Transport and eventually became a spray plane pilot. Sadly, he died tragically a few years later when he flew into a tree.

After I got my license, many of my flights were with Anthony, my cousin, who was fearless and a good companion on the runs to the Playboy Hotel and Montego Bay. On one cross-country flight, I decided to fly up the Yallahs valley and go over the top of Blue Mountain Peak. At an elevation of seventy four hundred feet and a mere ten miles from the coast, it was a steep climb for an aircraft that barely made six hundred feet per minute. The wind was blowing from the north that December morning as we entered the gorge of the Yallahs River from the south, causing a downdraft on the lee side of the mountain. Already deep into the valley, I glanced at the altimeter to see that we were in fact losing altitude. A quick turn put us back over the sea where I did a climbing spiral to eight thousand feet and then headed towards the mountain. After a buffeting by the mountain wave, we finally crossed the peak in clear weather, dipping a wing in greeting to a group gathered at the peak, facing the sunrise in apparent prayer. The north side of the mountain was seldom clear of clouds but it was that day. The low sun angle accentuated the sharp ridgelines and threw off a matchless shadow effect. We glided over to Manchioneal on the north-eastern corner of the island, turned west over a shoreline foaming with the north wind-driven breakers and soon landed at St. Margaret Bay airstrip. Later that day we took off and headed to Montego Bay, flying over the changing sea hues of the north coast. After lunch and a swim at Doctor's Cave Beach, we headed back to Kingston. The cloud cover had built up over the Cockpit Country, but not expecting low cloud bases in the winter months, we set out on the direct route to Kingston late that afternoon. The deeper we flew into the ominous Cockpit Country, the closer the cloud bases pressed towards the mountain peaks. Having no night or instrument rating, I was soon faced with the decision of spending the night at Montego Bay or pressing on. Not wanting to turn back, I foolishly decided to fly over the top of the cloud layer and entered another spiral climb. At ten thousand feet, the altitude where one needed to use oxygen, we were still not clear of the tops and I decided to fly on instruments through the clouds. This was very nearly a fatal decision. The Piper Colt had only two gyro instruments, an artificial horizon and a turn/bank indicator – insufficient for instruments flying. And I had no rating, nor for that matter experience flying only on instruments. In a very high percentage of cases of non-instrument rated pilots flying into clouds, they die because they become disoriented, don't believe their instruments, stall and fly into the ground. I believed the instruments and we somehow used dead reckoning to figure out when to descend through the clouds to set up an approach for Kingston. I went for my instruments rating after that episode and still wonder at the angel that took us through the clouds that evening.

"Six Yankee Juliet Charlie Xray, are you flying down the taxiway, sir?" the radio crackled from the tower.

"Negative, tower!" answered my check pilot Bobby Dixon as he flew a few inches above the taxiway after turning off the far end of the runway, in a hurry to get home. We had just returned from a check flight that included short field landings at Caymanas landing strip and a hilarious 'shooting up' of a train at Heartlands. The former WWII pilots were always re-testing their skills and many of them would have a lot of fun with these little diversions. Dixon was to check me out for solo flight later that month. A month after that, he was killed in a senseless crash at the approach to the runway at Kingston. This was in clear sight of the Jamaica Flying Club membership and right in front of the clubhouse one Sunday morning. He had survived the war to die at the hands of a student who apparently froze at the controls, broke the undercarriage in a hard landing and rolled the plane. The wing wrapped around the single door of the Piper Colt and left its occupants dangling but unhurt in their harnesses. The firemen rushed to the site and in an attempt to get them out of the wreckage cut through a wing strut holding the fuel line, setting off a ferocious fire. They burnt to death.

Jack Tyndale-Biscoe was an aerial photographer who plied his trade from an old tail-dragger airplane. Jack was known for taking pictures while in a steep turn, hanging out the window to get a clear shot without the obstruction of the struts. He would control the plane with his legs, since he seldom had a co-pilot on his photo runs. I flew with Jack twice and saw this at first hand. One Saturday morning while I was hanging around at Wings Limited, Jack drove up, loaded his camera into his plane and asked if I wanted to go with him to Bernard Lodge airstrip. Apparently someone, in attempting a landing, had strayed in a crosswind, mowing down a strip of banana trees. The insurance company had called Jack to take photos from the air and from the ground so that the reinsurer could see the wreckage. He dutifully unlatched the left window, stuck his upper body and camera out, and just then remembering that I was there, asked me to fly the plane.

Many years later, in about 1974, I was asked by one of the American Directors of the corporation where I worked to fly him around the island. This was a tricky situation given that this gentleman, a retired United States Air Force General was a personal friend of our Chairman and of CIA Director at that time, George Bush. General Andrews had met these men during WWII, when he flew pathfinder missions. The survival of pathfinder pilots was low and he was physically isolated from the bomber pilots, living in his own tent, so that they would not have to be traumatized by his loss in a dogfight.

He was a short, loud and confident man who I felt sure would want to take control of any airplane and I was worried about that. He walked around with a billfold laden with black and white photos showing damage to his airplane, sustained after about every mission as he dropped flares on targets for the bombers. Many of these photographs showed lines of bullet holes stitched across his Lightning twin engine airplane, doubtless from German fighters. He would flip the wallet open, spreading the photos out as he recounted his war days. How could I, a young manager in the company, refuse a war hero and company Director if he decided he wanted control of the plane? He had already given me his flight plan, which included landing at Boscobel to visit the Playboy Hotel before picking up his commercial flight in Montego Bay. I knew he would be drinking; I knew he was not rated to fly this particular airplane and I knew that he would make me give him control of the airplane from the right (co-pilot) seat. It then struck me that I would have to hand him off to my friend Freddy Ramson, who was by then flying for Wings Limited, who would be less restrained to refuse to give control of the airplane to General Andrews. I called Freddy and described General Andrews' personality to him. He later told me that he decided to use an airplane with only left hand side controls; Earlsy had the right hand side controls taken out to make space for flower shipments she flew out of the mountains. Freddy said that Andrews was indeed quite tipsy by the time they arrived in Montego Bay and had bitched the whole way about not getting to fly the airplane. Freddy did not give a damn.

These ex-USAF pilots remained lifelong friends, just like the ex-RAF pilots from Jamaica, and many became business owners and CIA country managers. Being a Director of an international company gave perfect cover for CIA operatives. General Andrews went on to found the first independent long distance telephone company in the USA, selling it a few years later for forty five million dollars.

In 1965 two of the ex-RAF officers in the Jamaica Flying Club, John Harrison and Garth Drew purchased a kit plane, a Pitts Special, and over the next year built it in Drew's garage in Kingston. The hedge had to be taken down to get the completed plane out on to a flat bed truck owned by yet another WWII pilot, Derek French. All these WWII types flew the Pitts, which was an aerobatics biplane. They were able to relive their war days in the Pitts and found new camaraderie.

These men and women were of a selfless generation. They survived a war where many of their companions did not and lived on with a joie de vivre that was contagious and magnificent. They became leading businessmen and never forgot their flying days.

Chapter eighteen

Broken Bulrushes

*T*he river erupted in a huge dome of swamp mud and debris, shot up past us and then fell in a torrent on and around us. "Great shot Jos!" shouted a grinning Robin, nervously hiding his terror as we clung to the swaying tree, shaken to its roots by the blast of the dynamite. We slithered down on wobbly knees and started gathering the mullet that were either quivering on the bank of the stream or swimming on their sides in circles in the muddy water.

Josiah the Rastafarian was the only hunter that I ever met in Jamaica. Robin and I met him in about 1967 on one of many fishing trips into the Guts River area in southern Manchester. Despite the obvious differences, we were to form a close friendship over the years. Josiah used dynamite as his weapon to hunt for fish and manatee in the years prior to our acquaintance and had been doing this well enough to make a living over a period of fifteen years.

We first met at the small shop in Guts River village, one of the ubiquitous corner shops found in rural areas where one could find everything from grocery items to fish hooks. There was always a crowd of idle men at the shop, even in the middle of the day and the commotion centered on the bar area where, in loud rum talk, the fishermen told tales of their morning's exploits. Josiah was buying groceries for his small shack in the swamp and we ran into him as we were buying supplies for the days spear fishing. A dignified looking, rake-thin, middle aged Rastafarian with few teeth but a broad smile, we were greeted with the traditional "I and I welcome the bald 'ead to our likkle village." That very day he shared his story with us.

"I-man use to kill cow, yu know," he said, looking pensive and tracing circles in the bare sand with his big toe. Thinking he was some sort of cattle rustler, we wanted to hear more, only to realize as the story unfolded that he meant manatee, known in Jamaica as sea cow.

"When I see de cow dem feeding pon de sea grass, I an' I would go into de water but never deeper dan me wais'. Den I would pick one out an' t'row de dandimite pon 'im," he animated with a throwing motion. "If it neva ded I an' I would kill it wid me 'lass [cutlass] an' tie it wid mi rope an pull it pan de sea bank where 'a butcher it. De market woman dem from Mandeville always follow me and dey would buy de meat an' sell it 'a market. Yu know dat cow have t'ree type a meat? It have beef, it have chicken an' it have pork. De pork part unclean to I an' I so de woman dem butcher dat part fi mi so me no haf fi touch it!" he continued. "Police neva trouble me, yu know, since I an' I would always donate to dem cause! But dem times gone since Independence. Mi no know wha' happen to de cow dem, but dem stop come a' Alligator Pon." I wondered if he ever connected his hunting with the departure of the manatee. I also wondered with some bemusement whether the good people of Mandeville knew what they were eating.

With manatee wiped out, he moved on to fish. Since he had no boat, he would walk along the seashore from Milk River to Alligator Pond in search of prey. This stretch of coast was probably the most remote in Jamaica. To the east was the mouth of the Milk River with its excellent radioactive spa, and the black sand beach stretched in an arc for fifteen miles to Alligator Pond. There was a rough, unpaved coast road that hugged the foot of the hill, demarking a strange boundary between the large swamp that stretched out to the dunes at the shore and the dry hills that climbed up to Mandeville in the hills above. Every few miles, a large blue hole popped up next to the road where a spring surfaced, and the bulrushes and floating mats of water grasses would push in and encircle the blue holes. Where the streams made their way to the sea, there was a bordering growth of mangroves ending in the raised sand dunes defining the beach. The western end changed into grassy swamps that had shallower water and looked like the Florida everglades, a sea of bulrushes dotted with thousands of mature swamp palm trees. The slow flow of water sheeted into Alligator Pond Bay, where manatees were historically known to calve and feed.

Perhaps because of Josiah's methods, the amount of fish caught on our spear fishing expeditions began to dwindle, so we decided to ask him to guide us to a good spot. He took us about a mile east of Guts River to a point where a large blue hole showed a river rising from the dry, cactus covered limestone right next to the road. Then he headed into the swamp. With some trepidation, we followed a hidden path that took us over a tough trail through mud and mangrove roots for about five hundred yards. Here Josiah had his shack, on a little mound next to the crystal-clear river and about a hundred yards from the beach. "Plenty fish right ya so!" he declared, pointing to the sea. Slipping on our goggles and flippers, we plunged into the heavy surf and swam out a hundred yards, but the water was too murky so we headed back to shore. Climbing up the beach, we happened on a mass of fish scales with the largest about four inches in diameter and curiously took some up for inspection. "Chapong!" Josiah informed us, using the slang word for tarpon.

"Nobody don't eat tarpon, Jos. What you do with it?" Robin asked, somewhat quizzically.

"De Chiney man dem know how fi fix it up an' tek out de bone dem, yu know. Dem scrape de meat off de bone and ball up de flesh mek de fine bone dem stick out, den dem pull dem out and cook it up! I sell it to de same woman dem wey me used to sell de cow meat an' dem tek it to Mandeville where de Chiney dem buy it".

We then decided to try for the Calipever mullet we had seen on our way down the little river, but as soon as we slipped into the water, they rocketed off into the sea.

"Yu' naa ketch nuttin like dat!" Josiah snickered as he headed into his shack. "Mek I an' I show de bald head bwoy dem how fi do it!" He emerged a few minutes later with a lit spliff in his mouth and a brown paper bag in his hand. We walked over to a large tree hanging over the river and he clambered up.

"Unnu come!" he ordered, and we followed him up the tree to a branch about fifteen feet above the stream. By then the school of mullet had reappeared, each about five pounds, swimming vigorously to keep up with the flow, feeding on the moss that floated down the river. In one motion, Josiah lit the contents of the bag with the spliff, tossed it into the stream and hugged up the tree while shouting "'eng on!"

Following his instructions, we tried to comprehend what was happening. The boom echoed across the hills as we spat out the debris and mud and tried to shake the ringing from our ears. As we helped him gather up the stunned fish, the current swiftly cleared the mud from the stream and Josiah intoned "Same place me ketch wan big alligator last month. Fifteen foot lang. Mi sell it to Mr. Jim Gore from town fi fifty poun' and 'im put it ina 'im used car place fi eat de t'ief dem!" Jim Gore had a used car mart on Hagley Park Road in Kingston, surrounded by an eight-foot zinc fence and was rumoured to keep crocodiles as watchdogs.

Robin wondered at this. "Jos. You say fifteen foot? How you catch it and how you get it to the road?"

"Yout', Rasta no tell lie! I an' I put a dead chicken pon a big hook and tie it ova the river, bout one yard high, wid a piece a big chain. Nex' mawnin mi come out mi house an' him jus a quiet heng up by 'im mout'. Mi pay a yout two shillin' fi go a bauxite place an' call Mr. Jim an' im come same day wid t'ree man and 'im lang-back Lan' Rover. Dem tie up the alligator pon two long lumber and wi wrassle im out thru the river to di road. A dat dey money mi use fi buy di dandymite mi jus lick out!" he laughed.

As we emerged from the track through the swamp that day, I saw a bulrush next to the track that despite being broken had managed to straighten itself and grow upward. In a strange revelation I remembered Tolstoy's broken thistle in his final work, *Hadji Murad,* and how he saw that as a metaphor for the Russian people*:*

> *"In front of me to the right of the road I saw some kind of little clump, and drawing nearer I found it was the same kind of thistle as that which I had vainly plucked and thrown away. This "Tartar" plant had three branches. One was broken and stuck out like the stump of a mutilated arm. Each of the other two bore a flower, once red but now blackened. One stalk was broken, and half of it hung down with a soiled flower at its tip. The other, though also soiled with black mud, still stood erect. Evidently a cartwheel had passed over the plant but it had risen again, and that was why, though erect, it stood twisted to one side, as if a piece of its body had been torn from it, its bowels drawn out, an arm torn off, and one of its eyes plucked out. Yet it stood firm and did not surrender to man who had destroyed all its brothers around it..."*

This bulrush was an equally fitting metaphor for this survivor of the swamps and for all the gnawingly poor working class people in our island. Josiah had never gone to school. There was none within fifteen miles. He learnt his trade from watching others and likely never realized that he single-handedly altered the entire ecosystem along miles of seacoast. Here we had a diamond in the rough, a broken bulrush, who did what he did to survive in a hard but beautiful land.

Josiah remained a friend until we stopped fishing and every once in a while the British teachers who we dated from Bishops High School in Mandeville would drive down to Guts River to play dominoes with Josiah and his friends. They never felt anything but friendship. I often wonder what became of Josiah as he aged to the point where he could no longer find fish.

Rural poverty

Growing up in rural Jamaica where poverty was everywhere around us, there was a degree of poverty that I had not experienced before that day in 1964. Even though our family would have been classified somewhere in the 'lower middle income' percentile if we had been in the USA, in Jamaica of the mid-twentieth century we were considered a wealthy family. We had a ten year old car where most walked or rode donkeys and a lucky few traded up to bicycles. We were landowners where most lived in 'yards', a truly odd living situation where poor people were forced to live a sort of communal lifestyle simply to survive and many very young children ran around nude while mother spiffed up for dance hall every Friday night. But that was their only chance to have fun and dress up.

After leaving high school at seventeen years old, and having a considerable though short-sighted preference for cash over continuing education, mom got me a job as a teller at the local bank. Spanish Town of the mid-1960s was bereft of opportunity and one either worked at the sugar estates or in the bank. My mom saw me as an accountant; I saw no prospects in that. One of the large clients of my bank was Innswood Estates, a 5,000 acre sugar cane estate and factory. Innswood, like all the other eighteen sugar estates in the island, relied on farmers to supply about half the cane needed to reach profitability. The farmers ranged from large operations like the Cawleys, DuQuesnays and Handals with hundreds of acres of cane, all the way down to hill country farmers with less than an acre. The large farmers would be issued orders each week for the tonnage the factory would accept and they would be responsible for cutting and hauling the cane to the factory. Because of the efforts of the Prime Minister at the time, Sir Alexander Bustamante, smaller farmers were not excluded and Innswood would arrange to haul loads of under a ton.

The payment for cane was made in three separate tranches – the first was at a set rate per ton and was paid at the end of each month. The second payment was based on the average sugar content of that farmer's deliveries that month and the third payment was much smaller and based on the price that the estate received for rum made from the molasses. The third payment was usually made months later, always after the crop ended and when the factory had sold the rum. Even though it was small, it was what sustained many a farmer outside the harvest period as sugar cane is only reaped once annually. I was very familiar with the workings of the factory, having worked holidays in the chemistry lab measuring boiler water solids, esters in the raw alcohol and the sucrose content of the raw cane juice. That had been an interesting job as gathering samples took me to all areas of the factory where I could see the huge clanging rollers crushing cane, follow the juice through the evaporation pans where water was boiled off, through the centrifuges used to separate molasses from sugar and into the fermentery where the molasses was mixed with water and yeast then left to become alcohol. It was a loud, dangerous place and I loved it.

Aubrey Massias, the manager of the bank, was clever enough to negotiate a deal with Innswood where the bank would deliver the Third Payments in cash to the small farmers scattered through the hill country north of the estate. The bank would earn a fee for making the payments, would have security that the estate could not match, and as a bonus, I was sent along to encourage the farmers to open savings accounts and to turn over their payments as new deposits.

The bank hired a Land Rover for the week and we set off with an armed guard to make payments in an area north of Old Harbour. I could not believe that anyone in Jamaica could farm in that arid, steeply sloping country, but there were parcel-sized farms clinging to the dry hillsides with just a few roots of desiccated cane visible. I was filled with a deep empathy for these farmers, especially when I saw one old guy hobbling up to the road from his shack down the hillside just to collect the few shillings I had for him. I could not in any good conscience open an account and take sustenance from this poor man; I reached into my own pocket instead and gave him a few shillings from my small wages.

I was so deeply affected by the struggle that these poor farmers must have faced each day just to feed themselves that I was unable to bring myself to even offer to open an account. Mr. Massias no doubt viewed me as a failure as a salesman, but I had not been raised by my parents to take advantage of those weaker than we were. I continue to suffer that infirmity and have dragged it with me through my business life.

This all played out in the 1970s, where well-meaning, populist politicians sought to redress centuries of inequality in the island and introduced a blend of socialism with its roots in African self-help theory. Ironically, the experiment resulted in a flight of capital and managers, followed by currency devaluations and inflation that visited more hardship on the heads of the very people that it was supposed to help.

Chapter nineteen

Scuba Do!

P aul Pasmore was a long-time friend who always had interesting ideas that were not always clearly thought out. One of these ideas was to make his own scuba tank and have a friend, Eric Millard, test it out.

We were hanging out at the Pasmore home in Stony Hill one Friday evening watching the TV show 'Flipper' when Paul first came up with this crazy plan, perhaps inspired by the divers in the show. After rummaging through his dad's garage, he came back in excitedly and announced that the problem was solved and that the three-gallon fire extinguisher would make the perfect scuba tank. He set about discharging the extinguisher, creating a huge cloud of dust that covered most of the little town of Stony Hill. With that inconvenience out the way, he washed out the empty tank, and after giving some engineering thought to how the air would be released, he arrived at a brilliant solution; the diver would keep the nozzle in his mouth and work the trigger every time he needed air. This all seemed perfectly logical and workable to us at the time, perhaps aided by the quart of Appleton rum we had just consumed.

The next morning I took the bus back up to Stony Hill as an interested observer of the field testing of the device. Paul borrowed his mom's car and with Millard selected as the guinea pig, we headed down the hill to Constant Spring. Gas stations in Jamaica always had air pumps with air pressure pre-select knobs and we pulled up to charge the tank. Having no idea how much pressure to put into the tank, Paul decided that 100-psi sounded about right since it was a nice round number.

He decided that Cable Hut beach was the right venue for the trials since it was always infested with girls and this would showcase his inventiveness. Half an hour later, we pulled into the parking lot and Paul rigged up the tank with a few belts and straps that he had scavenged from his dad's closet. We then hoisted the contraption onto Millard's back and he walked awkwardly down to the black sand beach, with goggles and flippers in hand. A crowd gathered in minutes while I took a few pictures for posterity (or was that obituary?) of Millard in the full regalia of Aquaman. Kicking out the flipper blades, Millard then waddled awkwardly into the surf. Adding to the suspense, he then very deliberately washed out the goggles, donned them, put the nozzle mouthpiece between his teeth and dived into an incoming wave.

The mouthpiece detached from the hose the instant he squeezed the trigger and the hose thrashed about as fiercely as a beheaded snake as he kicked furiously trying to submerge. This was extremely fortunate; since there was no regulator to de-pressurize the  compressed air in the tank, it surely would have killed him instantly.

The buoyancy of the tank kept him on the surface for the seconds it took the air to exit the tank and that probably saved his life. It was a great show though, and provided the impetus for us to learn more about the mechanisms of scuba diving.

Fred Jornsen was one of the more experienced divers in the country and after hearing the humorous tale of Pasmore and Millard, he strongly recommended that we join the British Sub Aqua Club. At the time, British Sub Aqua met in an old house on Lady Musgrave Road just below King's House (the Governor General's official residence) and was mostly comprised of scuba enthusiasts who were British nationals. They held monthly meetings to discuss future dive sites and to bring in new members and we were inducted with no problems.

The certification was all done at the National Stadium pool complex and, as we were to find out, was quite rigorous. We had to pass a number of skills tests to get certified and although I was a good swimmer, it was to prove tough, primarily because, at 5'10" and only one hundred and twenty pounds, I had no natural buoyancy. The first test was to swim one hundred meters in less than three minutes with a ten-pound weight belt strapped around the waist. The second was to tread water for a full minute with arms above the head. The third was a simulated rescue where one had to swim about forty metres to someone who was mimicking a drowning person, swim them to the edge of the pool, pull them out and start resuscitation. My drowning person ended up nearly drowning me, just to show that this was not a simple matter and that drowning people actually do grasp at straws. I made sure to scrape him from chin to waist against the pool edge as I pulled him out, just to show that straws can grasp back. In another test, they threw a full set of diving gear to the bottom of the five meter deep diving pool and tested that you could dive down and put it all on. They added to the difficulty by putting a leaky regulator on the tank, forcing you to drink out the water instead of just blowing it out. Then there were training sessions on getting water out of lungs, about the bends, about the dangers of cave diving, etc. It was a lot more rigorous than the PADI certification used by the Americans, and as starters one could only dive to thirty feet.

Over the next year I went on three expeditions, each of which had its own interest. The first dive was at a place named God's Well on the parish border between Clarendon and Manchester. God's Well was in the oddest of locations and was the weirdest of places to dive. As a rookie, my task was mainly to lug equipment to the site from the cars, a distance of just a few hundred meters but in an extremely hot and arid place. God's Well is located a few miles from Milk River, on the road to Gut's River. It is on a parched plain of red dirt and thorn trees and is completely unmarked. After I had panted along the track under a load of tanks and ropes, a huge hole in the ground suddenly appeared in front of me. I walked gingerly up to the rim; it appeared to be about thirty feet wide in one direction and maybe sixty in the other. A few mid-sized trees grew on the southern edge and only at midday did the sunlight hit the surface of the water, a full forty feet or so down. It was eerie; the water surface was so still that even the dust and pollen floated and did not mix in.

Soon a rope was tied to the largest tree and I lowered myself to the small shelf that sat just above the water, forming something like a beach. Fred was the dive master on this expedition and he addressed us about the mission – to chart the walls of the sinkhole and to mark any caves or entrances. The equipment was lowered but Fred was too lazy to come down the rope and dove into the pool from the rim. I was in the water at the time and saw the plume of bubbles as he penetrated to about fifteen feet. It was nearly his last dive.

The practice was to have a buddy at all times, and in a confined place like this, there were always a few divers in the water should trouble arise. Fred and his buddy diver descended into the eerie depths as soon as the sun got overhead at noon and sunlight penetrated the depths. I swam around the perimeter and dove down to my thirty foot limit to observe them. The water column consisted of a layer of fresh water about ten feet thick sitting on top of salt water. It was less than a mile to the beach so this was to be expected but the surprise to me, was the fact that the two layers had such a sharp dividing line. They never mixed, even when you swam through the boundary. The water was freezing cold, as was all spring water, and after about ten minutes I was shivering and had to come out. Fred did not surface when he should have and anxiety overtook the group. One of the experienced divers quickly put on his gear and went down. About ten minutes later all three surfaced to cheers of released anxiety.

Despite telling us not to enter caves, Fred and his wingman did just that, stirred up the mud and lost sight of the way out. Luckily they did not panic; they held hands and felt their way around the cave until they found the entrance. This occurred ninety feet down, and they came close to having to decompress. God's Well turned out to be 165 feet deep, with a number of small caves deep down. After we plotted its dimensions, it looked exactly like a sock, narrowing down to a small 'toe'. I never volunteered to go on another cave dive – too eerie, too cold, nothing to see and too dangerous.

The next dive was in the open sea one at Braco in Trelawny. Braco boasted the clearest water in Jamaica, where visibility at two hundred feet was normal except when the nearby Rio Bueno was in flood. The water got deep very quickly so we needed no boats and simply drove up past the private airstrip (later to be destroyed by the Government because it was being used to ship ganja to the USA) and parked next to the rocky shore. It was a magnificent dive. At that time there was no hotel there and since it was on private land it had few visitors. We dove into a small cleft in the rocky shore, and thirty feet out we were in over two hundred feet of water. British Sub Aqua believed in conservation and never allowed any creature to be taken, so we focused on enjoying the dive. The area was teeming with fish and the vertical reef face was a wonder of sponges, anemones and brilliantly coloured fish and lobsters. These were mostly what we called 'chicken lobsters' which never seemed to weigh more than a pound. At first I thought that they were just juveniles but the dive master, a marine biology lecturer from the University of Miami stationed at Discovery Bay, told us that this was a completely different species.

It was a bit scary at first, diving in an area where there was no reef to protect us from sharks, but the dive master told us that sharks were not as aggressive as in the movies and that we had nothing to fear as long as there was no blood in the water. The University of Miami used this site for many of its dives and its divers had placed grids of string along the vertical reef wall so that they could document the creatures and plants growing in each area.

A few months later I went on my third dive at Blue Hole in Portland, and by that time I was certified to descend to sixty feet. The mission was mostly to explore and map the walls of this deep depression in the seabed. The depth had already been determined some decades earlier by lead weight so we knew that it was one hundred and seventy eight feet deep, but there were no good theories to explain how a hole that deep could be made so close to shore. This dive had all the potential for nitrogen narcosis, or even the bends, and since we did not possess the new helium mixes that were being used in deep commercial dives, we had to carefully control dive times for the bottom parties. My job was to take full tanks of air down to thirty feet and sixty feet. Others with deeper ratings took tanks down further to be used as decompression stops. The tanks were tied to a rope that had been extended into the deep and floated to a large buoy. The bottom party would stop on the way up at each station for a pre-determined period to purge the nitrogen from their blood.

After my job was done, a few of us swam around the perimeter of the blue hole, exploring down to our certified depth. A stream with a decent flow cascaded in on the southern end and since the area is hemmed in on three sides by the steep tree-covered banks, there was little direct sunlight hitting the surface and no discernible sea current to scour out the fresh water. Just as in God's Well, there was a shallow lens of fresh water sitting on top of the salt water and as you swam through it, there was a turgid zone where the water lenses met. The water was cold and it was eerie diving in shaded, deep water where you could not see the bottom. We soon exited the water for a few Red Stripes at the nearby bar. The bottom party was soon up and described a dense tangle of tree trunks sitting on a muddy bottom. Few fish were seen and yes, the depth was a full thirty fathoms.

I would dive every once in a while with the club but basically lost interest when our friend Fred died in a car crash about a year later. The club was mostly made up of older expatriates with different social outlooks, and we were not that comfortable socially in the group. Paul Pasmore soon went off to dive at Port Royal where National Geographic was exploring the sunken city. About two thirds of Port Royal sank into the sea during the 1692 earthquake and Paul was one of the contract divers hired to man the suction devices used to clear the mud from the ruins and to then search and document artefacts.

I would free dive for spear fishing after that, but found that I was not good at holding my breath; on expeditions with Andre DuQuesnay and his friends, I found myself sitting in the boat while they easily free dived to seventy feet. I really enjoyed diving, especially in the sea, but as the reefs of Jamaica deteriorated and the small jewelled reef fish disappeared, this became less enjoyable.

Chapter twenty

Hanging with Ian

I first met Ian in late 1964 at the King Street branch of the Bank of Nova Scotia. Ours was to be a friendship of many years where I was fishing buddy, drinking companion, counsellor and confidant. Over the years I have only had a handful of true friends and Ian was one of the closest. I had just been transferred from the Spanish Town branch where I had proved unmanageable; apparently, I was intolerant of slick managers. The manager may have seen some redeeming virtue in me, but it is more likely that he did not want to fire me and risk the loss of my father's account.

Ian had just returned from school in England and together with his mother, Edna, had moved in with her sister Mrs. Pike until they could find a rental house. Ian's cousin Reema was married to a manager at the Bank of Nova Scotia, and was able to land him a job in the bank, though at the most basic level – block boy. He was a 'runner' for the department that processed cheques and deposits and he was in constant motion, moving paper from the twenty-four tellers to the back office.

The first day at King Street was intimidating to me, this country boy of eighteen, since I knew no one there and felt a bit out of place among these sophisticated city slickers. Ian had obviously heard that I was a troublemaker, but more importantly found out that I lived on a farm. For some strange reason, city folks seemed to have an idealized impression of farm life. A couple of days later he invited me to his home and after hanging out for a while, though I was uncertain if I wanted to become friends, he invited himself to the farm for the weekend.

That weekend was to cement our friendship. Although I was content to go fishing in the irrigation canals and go to the beach with my parents, Ian talked me into letting him ride one of our mules. My brother Chris and I were accomplished bareback riders but Ian wanted a saddle. The mules were used to pull the dairy farm's milk cart that was used to supply Spanish Town shops, and no matter how many times I told Ian that these mules had never been ridden with a saddle, he wanted to try. Despite deep misgivings, I managed to corral one of the more spirited animals, and, after a bout of kicking and prancing, was able to get a saddle on the beast. One of the tricks that I was to later find out was that these wily animals inflate their bellies while one is tightening the girth strap so that it later becomes loose. Well, this animal had that trick up its sleeve. As soon as Ian mounted, it took off at a dead gallop headed for a patch of brambles. It started to prance and in five seconds flat the saddle, with Ian still clinging to it, had slipped forward over the animal's front shoulder, and I was faced with the hilarious sight of this centaur headed for the bushes. Ian and saddle were ingloriously deposited in the thorns. After I retrieved my new friend from the thorn bushes and calmed down the mule we had a good laugh. He never again asked to ride a mule.

Manly Pursuits

Neither of us was accomplished in the finer arts of attracting women, though we tried gallantly, so we spent time on other pursuits with the hope that this would improve our chances. The first task was to bulk up our bodies. I was all of 120 pounds on a 5'10" frame, while Ian was about 6'2" and weighed about 140. We found an outdoor 'gym' in the back of a decrepit car repair yard, where most of the weights seemed to have been adapted from car parts. The round weights were gears from discarded transmissions and flywheels. The bars were evidently old axles. Tension springs were fabricated from old car seat springs and the odd truck drive shaft was pressed into use as a squatting weight. The gym was recommended by Bunny Grant, a Jamaican lightweight boxing champion and it was on Elliston Road – a rather depressed area next to the army camp. Bunny was later to come on spear fishing trips with us. He had the theory that if he could face a shark then boxing opponents would instil no fear.

The first session turned out to be the last. We did triple the workload recommended by Bunny, after we decided that we would accelerate the program so that within a few weeks we could add a minimum fifty pounds of muscle each. Unsurprisingly, we could not drag ourselves out to work the next day and decided that weightlifting was too hard. Some other method of attracting chicks would have to be found.

We then felt that we would become manly warriors by excelling at spear fishing; how difficult could that be? We envisioned the photos in the sports page of *The Daily Gleaner,* with us standing on a dock next to some poor shark that was unfortunate enough to come too close to us. We shopped at Andrew H.B. Aguillar, the city's pre-eminent sports shop; where else would we get equipment worthy of our virility? Goggles, flippers, weight belts and spear guns were procured at a cost of about a month's wages, and that very afternoon after work, we started practicing our technique. The pool at the Terra Nova Hotel was the closest body of water to Ian's home, so for a fee of five shillings we donned our equipment, scared away the few tourists that were in the water and started our training.

We turned out to be as accomplished at killing fish as we were at attracting girls. Our first open sea expedition was to the old Royal Navy coal wharf at Port Royal. We borrowed Mrs. Mitchell's Morris Mini Minor, making sure that the fishing equipment was conspicuously displayed for all to see and drove to Port Royal. The problem with Port Royal was that the water was murky on the harbour side and after we launched backwards in style from the wharf into the water, Ian lost his mask and spent the next ten minutes searching for it on the sea floor. We did not try that particular back-flip water entry method shown in the movies again, as experience had taught us that it stings the back and tears off one's goggles. Once in the water, visibility was about four feet and after nearly getting shot in my flipper by Ian who thought he saw a parrotfish, we decided that our failure to shoot even one fish was because there were none there. Or, that they saw us coming like the sheriff in a western and just took off.

Deciding that we needed to go further afield to find fishing grounds that had not yet been plundered, we made arrangements with my cousin Robin to stay at a beach house that belonged to one of his parents' friends at Roselle in St. Thomas. Robin brought along a retinue of young ladies to witness our prowess, after which he theorized we would have our way with them. These beautiful young ladies from England and Ireland were teachers at a girl's boarding school in Mandeville, Robin's hometown. Mandeville was in the mountains and thirty miles from the nearest beach, so Robin had no problem negotiating terms for these three to stay at the beach house with us. Little did he know that they had learnt well from their mothers and were skilled in the art of fencing, gently parrying all advances. They were also gracious, and made no complaint when we arrived to find that Mr. Randall did not in fact have a beach house, but had moved an old city bus onto the beach, put it on blocks and put a few beds in it. There was no bathroom and no privacy and in baseball terms, we struck out. We did no better in the water, as the sea was rough the entire weekend, being one of the few sections of Jamaica's coastline without a reef to block the waves. After being rolled over in the surf a few times, a new game plan was put in place. We would pursue river fishing instead.

Robin had grown up in St. Thomas and decided that we would visit the Bath Spa and its river. After some deep soaking, the spa would hopefully relax these uptight girls while we conquered huge mountain mullet in the Plantain Garden River. Unfortunately, the girls were more attracted to the Rastamen providing a freelance massage service by the riverside and we decided that it was prudent to preserve our dignity by leaving early. Our catch for the day amounted to a few 'janga', or pincer less shrimp, averaging two inches in length. These girls were good sports though, and in the spirit of pursuit, let us continue to try our hand at seducing the unattainable in exchange for allowing them to come on future trips.

Eventually we were to become better at the sport and just to prove to ourselves that we could at the very least feed ourselves, we later arranged a weekend-long trip to Pelican Cay. This time we carried no food. Accompanied by the teachers, we set off in a hired canoe from Old Harbour Bay late one Friday afternoon, with five crates of Red Stripe beer, an old bucket and two hundred pounds of ice. The fisherman dropped us off on the beach and we immediately buried the ice and the beer in the sand and set up our hammocks in the mangrove trees.

This time Robin had brought along a friend from boarding school, the son of a British Lord, who had been sent to a far-off private school in Jamaica to get him away from the influence of drugs in England. 'Big' Pelican Cay was about five miles offshore and about two hundred yards long; it had a beautiful beach on the shore-facing side and a rocky reef on the seaside. It was uninhabited, with a dense stand of scrubby trees, but we knew from earlier trips that, hidden in the trees, there was a stand of ganja that the local fishermen had planted for their own use. Well, the English aristocrat found this weed and went missing the entire weekend. He steeped some in gin and set about smoking whole branches by stuffing them into a beer bottle whose bottom he had knocked out, pulling smoke through the bottleneck. We never saw him except when he left his hammock to eat, and he was constantly surrounded by a pall of smoke and the crackling of the ganja seeds and branches he was too lazy to remove.

Our fishing was outstanding. The fisherman came by in the mornings and took us to spots where we saw all the lobster and fish we could handle. The water was spectacularly clear, and one of our favourite spots was an old, wrecked wooden ship. The water was about thirty feet deep, and as we dove down we could see dozens of lobster antennae moving within the old ballast stones of the wreck. Just like in the movie Blue Lagoon, we would come ashore with a full catch and the girls would gather driftwood, make a fire, catch a bucket full of sea water and cook the lobsters. We traded the fisherman most of the fish against the rental of his boat and only kept a few boxfish (called buck-buck by the fishermen in the area). The boxfish were all about a pound or so in weight and had a curious triangular cross-section. Instead of scales, they had a hard shell with hexagonal segments, with only the fins and lips sticking out. After gutting, they were put into the coals and made a delicious meal. The beers went down well as we then sat on the beach and watched the sun set.

Sunburn was inevitable after two days of non-stop spear fishing, especially since we were dressed in trunks all the time, and we slept painfully in corded hammocks. Ian added to his misery by shooting a large leopard ray that had been getting too curious and swimming towards him. It took off through his legs, flipping him over and eventually snapped the spear cord, bruising his leg in the process. He had no spare spear.

In 1966, we decided to try our hand at fishing in Grand Cayman and were able to convince my brother Chris and his medical schoolmate, Ronnie DuQuesnay, to come along. We convinced them that no fewer than half of all adult Caymanian men were commercial sailors who only returned home once or twice yearly, leaving a nation of frustrated women and unfished seas. The BWIA flight was uneventful and in this earlier era, we were able to take our spear guns on board as hand luggage with no problem. Cayman airport was a shed with a zinc-covered table pretending to be the Customs area. We had the lone taxi man take us to the home of a Mrs. Ebanks who rented rooms at one pound sterling per night. She turned out to be a great hostess, cleaning and cooking the fish we brought home. Having little money left over after the plane fare and boarding costs, we decided to get around by rental bicycle. At that time Cayman had only two hotels on the seven mile beach, and almost no one had boats to rent. We would ride along the shore on our bicycles, and if we found a spot that looked promising, we would get in the water and try. The first day we ended up on the south western corner of the island, place called South Sound. Here we saw a diminutive canoe set on chocks. The area was almost devoid of habitation, but we could see one sandy, conch-lined path through the beach morning glories. This led to a small house, so we knocked on the door and were able to borrow the canoe from an elderly gentleman. The canoe could only fit three, so my job was to flipper behind the boat, pushing it to the reef. The problem was that the current running inside the reef was probably four knots, or about the speed of a fast walk, and we were quickly drifting away from the reef. We all got into the water and pushed and managed to get to the reef, next to an old lighthouse. The reef surface was about a foot underwater with breakers crashing over it but we were able to get to the outside and each made our daily limit of two lobsters and maybe twenty pounds of snapper. Ian ended up being flung by the waves onto fire coral and spent most of the afternoon with huge welts all down his side and leg. He persisted though, until, on the way back to shore, we were all driven into this tiny boat by an absolutely gigantic barracuda. Barracuda are always hanging around as one spear fishes, but would take off if you gestured towards them. This one took a fish off my spear and glided closer with an open mouth even as I shouted and rushed towards it. It was so large that it had green moss growing on its back.

By the second day, the bicycles were becoming a burden. It was impossible to carry all the catch on bicycles, but more to the point, it was impossible to ride into the strong trade winds. We then scratched up enough cash to rent a 1960 Ford Falcon from an unlikely owner, Hummingbirds, and on our second day decided to try the eastern tip of the island. There was a single small hotel there, next to a little village. The reef at this point was about a mile offshore, and after an hour of shooting small fish around the coral heads that dotted the water inside the reef, we decided to find larger fish. A local lad was bribed to take us in his dad's boat to the reef and to a very large sunken ship that was sitting on top of the reef. Getting to the wreck was easy, the water being fairly calm inside the reef, but as we approached, the waves were mountains crashing into the wreck. We found an old rope ladder and foolishly climbed up perhaps forty feet to the shuddering deck. The rollers were relentless on this windward side of the island and had taken out the hull on the seaward side of the wreck. As each wave came thundering in from the purple-blue deep, it would roll entirely through the hold and hit the lee side, sending up a towering mass of spray. We would have been shredded had we tried to get into the water on the outside of the reef, so we contented ourselves with shooting small fish at the coral heads and trading some for a few beers and lunch at the small hotel. Surprisingly few Caymanians fished in those times.

The third day saw us drive to the north eastern tip of North Sound, the large bay on the northwest corner of the island. The fishing was not that good, but we found countless conchs in the shallows and decided to take some to Mrs. Ebanks so she could cook them for us, adding to our virility. On the way back, Ian drove the car over a large rock and tore off the engine mounts, sending the engine into the radiator. This was to be the first of many cars that Ian was to wreck over the years.

Cayman had its share of characters and over the next few days we were to encounter our share of them, including a very friendly Jamaican ganja runner who insisted on hanging out with us and a ten year old girl, blond and barefooted, on a bicycle sucking on a Pabst Blue Ribbon beer. While in a bar one night, we were approached by two absolute legends of the night. One introduced herself as Iron Front and her friend as Sugar Wee. We graciously declined the invitations they extended to us. Our theory that Caymanian sailors rarely returned home was disproved as we also encountered a deranged sailor-husband who returned to the island unexpectedly to find his wife dancing with one of our group.

We returned the car as late as possible the night before our departure, in a vain attempt to escape the consequences of the earlier wreck. Mrs. Hummingbird was waiting for us at the airport, and extracted for repairs all the money we had left. On such a small island, everybody knows what is going on.

Another memorable expedition was the time we camped out overnight with June Ryan and her niece at Drax Hall so that we could go fishing early the next morning. This was at the famous Columbus Cove, which was an idyllic spot with coconut trees draping the shore, complete with a burbling brook tumbling into the cove. The weather was fine and a warm breeze was blowing that evening as we bedded down on a blanket in the open. By 10:00 p.m., the heavens opened up and we had to spend the rest of the night in wet clothes in the car. To make matters worse, the morning broke with a stiff north wind that stirred up the sand so we could not see a thing underwater.

By 1967 or thereabouts we were a bit more successful in getting girls to go with us on trips to the beach and by then had wheels and could venture further afield. Negril Beach at the western tip of Jamaica became a popular spot, since it was excellent for both spear fishing and hanging out and watching the sun set. The drive from Kingston to Negril was about five hours. One weekend we drove separately to Negril and after being driven out of the water onto the honeycomb rocks of Bloody Bay by a very, very large shark, I decided to leave early. Ian stayed on with the girl he had brought from Kingston, only to have his car broken into and his clothes and wallet stolen. Ian had a habit of not filling up his gas tank when he should and showed considerable salesman skills in successfully begging money from strangers to buy gas for the drive home. I can see him now, turning over his eyes as he negotiated.

The last time I went spear fishing with Ian was in about 1970 at Guts River in Manchester. By this time I was married and my wife, Olivene, came along for the ride. Ian was my dear friend but he was always an accident waiting to happen. He was either burning his shirt with a cigarette, losing his keys, crashing his cars or simply tripping and falling on furniture. On this outing, we travelled in Ian's Ford Galaxy, and true to form, he managed to lock the car keys in the trunk. The area around Guts River was stark, cactus filled and very hot. It was one of the most remote areas in Jamaica and there we were, stranded. The decision was made to go shoot some fish and deal with the key problem later. The spring that forms Guts River is a strong flow of icy cold water flowing swiftly from a twenty-five foot vertical crack that is only about five feet wide. We had little luck that day. The fish had obviously been fished out – the water was so clear that fish were literally just sitting in a bowl waiting to be caught. The key problem was resolved by using a knife to screw off the twelve inch, circular taillight and fishing out the keys through the gap.

The Baker's Dozen

Scotia Bank, King Street was one of the largest employers in the city, and by 1965 we had formed a loose group of 13 or so singles. This 'Bakers Dozen' was wholly dedicated to touring and having fun. It was a fun group that included about an equal number of boys and girls and was surprisingly friendship-based with few, if any, intimate relationships. We went on trips to Blue Mountain Peak, Montego Bay and Negril. Some of the people in the group were June Ryan, Helen Senior, Sandy Sasso, Christian Smith, Helen Barker, Johnny Johnson and Ken Carby. June's brother George's house was a favourite gathering place for the group and was to yield marriage and grief over the years. Claudia, George's wife had two sisters and her mother living there with her. Helena, the younger sister, was to become Ian's wife. Carol, the other sister died tragically in a car accident; June died at the hand of her husband and George himself died young of cancer. Ian sadly now joins them.

Transport was always a problem since few of us had cars, but through trickery and guile we were always able to borrow cars and to find places to stay for the weekend. In those days, the auto dealers would sometimes let prospective buyers take cars out 'on demonstration', and one of us was always a prospective buyer. On one trip to Montego Bay, we took a Mini Moke on demonstration from a car dealership and George had to fill in to provide overflow transportation. A Mini Moke was a Mini Minor with the sides and top cut off and replaced with something looking like a canvas awning on poles. Helen Senior was to arrange housing in Montego Bay, so she asked her brother to lend us his house, but when we got there, it was a one bedroom house for thirteen people. This was not to be a problem, though. The mattress was taken off and three or four slept on that, four more slept on the spring and the rest of us split up between the two cars, with me on George's car roof.

One night we went to a famous nightclub in Montego Bay named Yellow Bird. We knew the owner, Billy Vernon, one of the best guitarists in the island, and on one of his band breaks we asked if one of our group could play. Pat Jolly, who fifteen years later married my sister-in-law, was then a guitarist in a band from May Pen and we pushed him to the stage where he brought the house down. Hearing the commotion, Billy returned early to the stage to preserve his reputation. Knowing the bottle charge for rum was high, we had the girls smuggle bottles in under their skirts. Ian managed later to trip over his dance partner; he came crashing into our table and broke two of the precious bottles of smuggled rum.

Blue Mountain trips were physically difficult and took lots of planning – a skill none of us then possessed, so it fell to the branch accountant, an Englishman named Mike Hearst, to make the necessary arrangements. Mike was a bit older than the rest of us and was married, though his wife seemed to forget this from time to time. We got some sleep at Whitfield Hall, and just after midnight woke to hike the seven miles to the peak to see the sunrise. Less than a mile up the trail, Mrs. Hearst started propositioning each of the men, in turn. Mike, as branch accountant, was the boss of all of us, so this was something of a dilemma. We somehow evaded her and reached the peak to see a most glorious sunrise. Surprisingly, Ian was one of the strong shoulders that carried many of the weaker women up the trail, since he was by then up to two packs of cigarettes per day, the root of his eventual demise.

The last trip by the 'Dozen' was to Sunnyville, my grandparent's house in Hanover. This was set on a mountaintop and had a glorious view from a sweeping veranda that surrounded the house. My uncle had inherited this house and kept it as a private fishing camp, but was happy to lend it to us as a base for visits to Negril and Montego Bay, and side trips to Fort Charlotte in Lucea. This was by far the most interesting and enjoyable of all the trips for many reasons, not least of which was that it was a four bedroom house, so no one had to sleep on car tops or other inconvenient places.

The Cars

Ian had a propensity to wreck perfectly good cars. In the first five or so years that I knew him, he had at least seven serious wrecks. None was the other driver's (or tree's) fault and Ian was seldom the worse for wear. The first was his mom's Mini Minor. We had planned to visit the beach in Port Antonio one Saturday morning so Ian set off to pick up the girls, planning to then swing back to pick me up. He never showed up. After about an hour, a mutual friend came by my place to pick me up to drive Ian's car to the garage while Ian was stitched up and had his finger splinted. On his way to collect the girls, he managed to run into the back of a city bus that had stopped at a bus stop on a perfectly straight stretch of road. When he saw that he had no space to stop, he yanked up the hand brake to try and spin out and only succeeded in squashing in the passenger side of the car.

His mum replaced the Mini Minor with a 1963 Ford Corsair GT and a month later we spent the afternoon at Victoria Pier drinking beers. After filling the large round table with empties, it was decided that he would drive me home to Spanish Town. Along the way, he decided to see how fast the car would go in third gear. I shouted to him to slow down when the speedometer nearly hit 100 mph in third but it was too late; the damage was done, leaving us stranded on Spanish Town main road with a blown engine.

The next car was a large American one that was probably bought to put sheet metal between him and what he was about to crash into. A group of about four of us went to the famous Thursday night dance at Club Maracas in Ocho Rios and just before dawn decided to drive back to Kingston. I drove separately and decided to return cross-country via

Mount Diablo. Ian decided to go back on the north coast and through the Junction Road. Anthony, my cousin, was travelling with Ian and fell asleep immediately, but by the time they reached twelve miles up the road, he awoke to the sound of grass swishing past the car – Ian had fallen asleep and had driven into a pasture. Somewhat late, Anthony's survival instinct kicked in and he persuaded Ian to drop him off at a friend who lived in Oracabessa. The next morning, I got a call from Port Maria. Ian had been driving in the rain, too fast, and upon approaching a 'Y' junction in the road could not decide on which leg to follow so he went straight. He ended inverted in a river, having taken out the water supply to Port Maria. How he survived that unscathed is a mystery, but he brushed himself off and walked in the rain to the Kong's house.

He then bought a Triumph Dolomite and survived two crashes in that one. After about a month of ownership, he called me from home one morning, and in a shaky voice said that he had found what appeared to be bullet holes in his car and could not recall how this might have happened. There were also smudges of green paint, and he was terrified that he had hit another car and left the scene. Within the hour, a mutual friend called me to complain that Ian had overtaken him at a high speed just as he was making a right turn. In swerving away, Ian had taken down a stretch of tall privet hedge and someone's green gateposts, and just kept driving. The 'bullet holes' were actually where the branches of the hedge had pierced the car body. The Dolomite was fixed, and six months later, after leaving a stag party, he ended up crashing into a tree by the Cholera Cemetery on Waterloo Road. Bleeding profusely, he was rescued by my cousin Steve who had left the party just behind him. This time he had to go to hospital for stitches, though not before Steve was instructed to scavenge the new 8-track tape deck. Steve had to go get Ian's mother, covered in his blood, and was greeted with hysteria by poor Mrs. Mitchell. Did he ever age his mother!

In 1967 we were to set a speed record from Kingston to Montego Bay. We were already in Montego Bay when Ian's car conked out. Mrs.

Mitchell's family was from the area and Ian knew a family that owned a rent-a-car business there. We were able to borrow an MGB-GT from the rent-a-car to go to Kingston to buy a part, which would be installed Ian's friend's mechanic when we returned. I drove this time. The plan was to leave the ladies overnight with friends and to return early Saturday morning. With a clear road, we were able to get from Kingston to the Montego Bay airport in two hours and seven minutes, with a delay for a tire change and a stop to put the top down for rain. That record was to stand until two years later when it was bettered by five minutes by a friend. This was my way of getting even with Ian for his insane driving, though it hardly seemed to faze him. We were impossibly crazy drivers and it is a miracle that either of us survived our youth, though I myself managed to avoid accidents.

Ian was always open to wagers, even impossible ones. One evening, we were visiting a family who lived in the foothills of Kingston and after a few beers, someone wondered if it was possible to climb that short hill on the other side of the road. For five pounds ($10), Ian agreed that in thirty minutes he would climb all three hundred feet to the top of Armour Heights, wave to us from there and then get back down. The hill was vertical and covered in a species of thorny bush with the unfortunate name of 'one way macka'. In other words, you can go in but you can't extricate yourself from the curved thorns. The intrepid climber set off through the neighbour's backyard, fending off the dogs along the way, and disappeared into the thicket. He had not returned within the thirty minute time limit, but we thought nothing of it until about an hour or so later; the neighbour's maid came running to tell us that this 'big white man' who recently ran through their yard had fallen off the hill and was lying motionless at the foot of the hill. Other than the hundred cuts from the one way macka's thorns, there was nothing that another pint could not help. We did not take his money.

The Early Twenties

We somehow survived our late teens and entered a new phase of life. Finally able to get dates, we would often double date, sometime with amusing or interesting outcomes. I recall a young lady and her sister starting at the bank in about 1967. She went on to become second runner up in the Miss Jamaica beauty pageant and we somehow ended up with dates with this pair. Pansy was not sophisticated, being of very religious parents and a rural upbringing. She was pretty but her accent was deep rural St. Elizabeth. In celebration of her pageant near miss, we decided that the elegant Myrtle Bank Hotel on the waterfront was appropriate. Myrtle Bank's elegance was of an earlier era, but it still had an aging glamour. It had a band, and the bandstand was on a dock over the water. Ian paired up with Pansy and I had her sister Violet on my arm as we sashayed onto the dock in full tuxedo to the strains of Kes Chin and the Souvenirs band. "I'll 'ave a screwdriver!" smiled Pansy, oozing confidence in her sophistication and worldliness. "Me too!" parroted Violet. We knew that they were on the way to insobriety and planned to keep plying them with vodka until their resistance faltered. We were thwarted yet again, when this flowered pair ended up blind drunk and sick, then unconscious. All we could do at that stage was take them home and carry them into their mother's house under violent verbal parental abuse. A week or so later, the Myrtle Bank Hotel burned to the ground. We had nothing to do with that.

The years rolled by and after I got married and left Scotia Bank, Ian moved on. For a time, he transferred out to Montego Bay. We saw less of each other as my kids arrived and then Ian and Helena got married. It was a great event at George and Claudia's house where I was called upon to be his best man and asked to hold off on the memories. So I write them now.

I transferred with my family to work and live in Trinidad and then Nassau and Ian moved back to England so we had even less contact, though we did keep in touch. I was able to introduce Ian to good friends we had in Nassau, Hugh and Cecile Pike. The Pikes were teachers in Nassau and were moving to England and coincidentally planned to move close to where Ian lived. They became best friends. On infrequent business trips to the UK, I would find time to visit and meet his daughters, Anna and Lisa. We enjoyed the walk in the woods behind his home and Ian would tell me that this was the happiest time in his life, though he still maintained a sometimes stern and tough demeanour. It was not a surprise to me that Ian was able to rise to Vice President of a large London bank and have the responsibility of billions of dollars traded daily with an unfinished high school education. It is a testament to the man's talent and his ability to work well with others. We kept in touch through email and I was happy to see that he was at last able to retire with a decent income so that he could do some of the things he always wanted to do. He was thrilled to crew on a boat from Tampa to Montego Bay in 2005 and we had started making arrangements to play some golf. Unfortunately, time did not allow. Farewell, my friend.

Chapter twenty-one

A Grave Misunderstanding

*A*fter our grandmother passed away in 1956, Sunnyville was left to our Uncle Cliff, but it was always available to the rest of the extended family. Cliff used it mostly as a fishing lodge, and whenever he was not there, he would willingly allow his teenaged nephews to use it. Clinton and Nancy were the live-in caretakers and whenever we wanted to spend a weekend, we could always depend on Nancy to greet us, shop for groceries, cook for us and generally mother us. Uncle Cliff, perhaps because he wore the parson's collar, had married Clinton and Nancy soon after he took over Sunnyville. This was a bit of a novelty among the labouring class in Jamaica.

My mother always believed that Clinton was a "worthless so-and-so" because she felt that he was responsible for grandma's early death at eighty-four years of age. Her theory was that Grandma called out to Clinton when the heart attack grabbed her but that he was just too "damned lazy" to immediately run the five miles to Lucea, the nearest town, to call the doctor. She adored Nancy but saw Clinton as the typical Jamaican labourer – irresponsible and only interested in the Friday night dance hall and impregnating as many women as possible and not "minding" the babies. The truth was that there was very little in these folks' lives besides work and whatever chance they had to dress up, they would do so to get some respect from their peers.

Clinton's responsibility was to take care of the property and Nancy's, the house. His tasks included herding the few cattle, planting and reaping yams, guarding the crops from theft and when the pimento crop came in, he climbed the trees and reaped the crop by breaking off the small branches that held the berries. He was about 6 feet 4 inches tall and well built, and in any social class would have been considered a very handsome man. He had a square jaw, great teeth, a trim muscular body, a good personality, was a great talker and, except for an accident of birth, could have been anything. In the mid 1960s, he must have been in his mid-thirties, and when we boys started visiting with girlfriends, he would hang out with us, drinking beer and playing dominoes.

On one particular trip in 1966, a group of four of us arrived at Sunnyville with intentions of yet again trying our hand at dating tourist girls in Montego Bay. Montego Bay was about twenty miles away and the plan was to try the nightclubs the first night and if we had no luck there, try the hotel bars on the next night. The days would be spent at Doctor's Cave beach, a favourite haunt of teenaged tourists as well as local middle class kids. This was to be a full court press since we had had no luck on previous jaunts and obviously the only reason was that we had not been trying hard enough. All our friends in Montego Bay boasted of numerous foreign romances and were we not as accomplished, handsome and desirable? Oozing with hormones, lacking in experience but confident of our success, we rolled into town like cowboys of an earlier century.

That first evening we boasted to Clinton and Nancy that we would not be there for dinner and quite possibly breakfast as well. We would be hitting the nightclubs. We then went off to our rooms to get ready. Drenched in Old Spice, all slicked out in our best clothes and with youthful enthusiasm we gathered at about 8:00 p.m. to set off to town. What a sophomoric sight we must have been. Clinton joined us on the verandah. He was dressed in a well fitting tweed jacket, a tie, tan pants and well-polished black shoes. "Ok, guys, where we heading first?" he asked. Now this was awkward. In the first place, he was not invited. Secondly, he was married. Thirdly, it would have been a social faux pas if Uncle Cliff and our parents heard that we had taken Clinton with us on a 'lime' as they would say in Trinidad – this 'familiarity' was just not tolerated by the older generation! Fourthly, but in retrospect most importantly, he was much more attractive than any of us and would probably end up with the girls – there was this well worn story that tourist girls came to Jamaica to sample what was taboo in their own segregated country.

Clinton was our pal but we were a product of our society, neither sufficiently courageous nor mature enough at nineteen to buck the system. We awkwardly told him that he could not fit into either of the two cars since we would doubtless each find a girl and need all the space. Jamaica was just as segregated as the USA, perhaps not so much racially but definitely socially. This incident was the result of a generational change overlaid on a society that still clung to colonial attitudes although it was itself rapidly changing to a modern society.

We were so troubled by our inability to deal with this that none of us scored that weekend. Clinton remained our pal. Perhaps he was more accepting of his social status than we thought, or he had simply been knocked down by life sufficient times to be able to take this in stride.

Chapter twenty-two

Wealth's Paradox

*I*n the summer of 1968, my simple world would intersect with one that was completely different from anything in my previous experience. Returning one Sunday from a weekend in Montego Bay, Robin and I had to make a stop in Ocho Rios where our girlfriends had an ***Alliance Français*** meeting. The Silver Sands Hotel was an older, privately owned, mid-sized establishment on the Ocho Rios hotel strip, sporting the art deco curves of the 1930s. The most exciting place in this unexciting joint was usually the beach bar.

The bar/dining porch area, to our chagrin, was virtually bereft of humanity. We were seeking a little harmless flirting with any young ladies of a foreign persuasion but only the manager, an obviously gay white Jamaican, and an elderly pink-haired lady were present. The manager fluttered over and started making conversation. It soon became clear that he was trying to set us up with the pink-haired matron. He confessed to us that the lady, a well-known heiress to a department store fortune, was a regular guest who rented half the hotel for three months each year. He pointed to the mini-cruise ship-sized yacht at anchor in the bay as evidence of the importance of this guest to his establishment. The house was evidently expected to supply regular male companionship. Since he was so insistent, and with a few hours remaining until the girls returned, we decided to get this pimp off our back and have a few drinks and some laughs. Little did we know what we had let ourselves in for.

After we allowed ourselves to be introduced to the lady, she immediately ordered a bottle of Don Perignon champagne for us and a strange pink concoction for herself. Sucking on a cigarette in a foot-long holder, she was drunk and loud, with a hacking cough that sounded like a death rattle. In a completely unexpected move, both her left and right hands reached under the table for our respective crotches. As we kicked back our chairs in surprise, she laughed an awful belly laugh mixed in with uncontrollable hacking, obviously impressed by her cleverness.

We learned that her family owned the largest department store chain in Canada, and she told us that she had all the money one could wish for, yet she was the loneliest person on God's green earth. She had been married numerous times but had yet to find happiness. She also told us that she was operating on one lung as the other had been removed a year earlier and she expected the lung cancer to return soon. A creature no doubt worthy of pity, she just wanted some company. We sat and chatted about nothing for the next two hours, thrice turning down cash inducements to accompany her upstairs. She had been hardened by a procession of loveless marriages, learning the hard way that men showed interested in her because of her wealth rather than for herself. No longer having interest in romance, she was now on a mission, using her wealth in feckless, physical pursuit of young men.

The girls returned from their meeting and we drove off, pensive yet sorry for this lost soul who apparently had all that life could offer except for the two most important things – health and the happiness that only love could bring. Perhaps, like the butterfly, one has to go through the struggle of emerging from a chrysalis' hard sheath to fully enjoy life. I learned an invaluable life lesson that day, imprinting the realization that unearned wealth and fame have their hazards as surely as does poverty. This was the first time we had been exposed to someone of truly great wealth and we had a hard time coming to grips with the reality of having everything yet having nothing.

Some twelve years later, I was at the Nassau Harbour Club in the Bahamas and while walking along the 'Millionaire Row' of yachts, stopped to chat with the captain of a boat I seemed to recall seeing moored in Ocho Rios Harbour that day in 1968. He told me that Mrs. X had died a decade earlier and that her daughter continued to use the yacht for cruises to the Bahamas, Monaco and other ports. Perhaps she was in pursuit of a lifelong romance with the perfect mate, or like her mother, she had given up and had settled for the relentless pursuit of pleasure.

Chapter twenty-three

The Swan

*A*s I walked into the tiny chapel at Rock Hall I was greeted by the most angelic sound wafting from the strings of an old violin in the hands of an even older black gentleman. Saint-Saëns 'The Swan' was so beautifully and elegantly played that it sent shivers right down my spine. Jamaica never failed to surprise and one could not have anticipated such a wonderful performance from someone that, from his appearance, would have had few opportunities to learn classical music. I sat there thinking back on the paradoxes life presents and how death can reveal these even to those who do not seek.

It was Uncle Dennis DuQuesnay's funeral here in the serene mountains of Jamaica. Where was his family? Where were the friends? The annual DuQuesnay Christmas party drew a crowd at least thrice that of the congregation.

Glancing around, I saw three of his five sons, his second wife but no daughters-in-law and only two of the fourteen grandchildren. The chapel was otherwise filled with folks I did not recognize, though after the service I discovered that they were mostly small farmers that Uncle Dennis had met in the 1960s when he was president of the Sugar Cane Farmers Association. They were humble men, probably all of another religeon who felt it a duty and responsibility to attend an old friend's funeral even after he had been out of touch for forty years. Few of the white gentry of Kingston, his school friends and social companions of an earlier era, saw fit to show up.

The DuQuesnays had originally come to Jamaica from France in the nineteenth century and had quickly established themselves in business, as professionals and in farming. Dennis married in 1939 and by 1944 had bought a cane farm on the outskirts of Spanish Town and about three miles from our farm. He carefully maintained his contacts among the business community in Kingston and even after he turned to farming still operated a bottle buy-back business, running trucks that would purchase empties from all over the island, reselling them to the beer, rum and soft drink bottlers. He had five sons, all born between 1941 and 1950, and the family was a pillar of the local Catholic Church. The boys went to the Catholic boys' school in Kingston and this allowed the family to retain links to family and friends in Kingston.

The annual DuQuesnay Christmas party was legendary. There were always over one hundred guests, most from Kingston. To us Virtues, it was the season's highlight, giving the boys a chance to flirt with the many pretty teenage girls and to show off newly acquired, if unconventional, dancing skills. Jamaicans never viewed alcohol as the moral and spiritual danger that it was perceived as in the USA, so it flowed freely and was available even to us mid-teens. One of the sideshows was a female DuQuesnay cousin from the USA who had the contrary habit of becoming quieter the more inebriated she became. Sober, she had a sparkling personality, vivacious and friendly, but when plied with drinks she became shy and withdrawn. It was an annual rite of passage to see how quickly she would go under.

The DuQuesnay house was set back well in from the Old Harbour Road, and had a swimming pool (we knew of few others in the parish) and a well stocked fishpond. It was a large, two-storey, concrete house set in a stately setting, surrounded by huge guango and eucalyptus trees. Dennis was well-off compared to the other farmers and was an astute and charming businessman. He was suspected of having an outside girlfriend in Kingston and this caused great, though quiet, consternation within the community. To me and all the boys he was a very friendly, gentle and kind man whom we respected and liked.

By the early 1970s the property had become very valuable. The town had advanced and a new highway was being built. The sale earned enough to buy farms for the two oldest sons, with a large sum left over. This was all invested in an upscale housing development in Kingston. The development was organized to provide houses for the three youngest sons, with the remaining profit targeted towards retirement. But dark shadows of socialism were emerging and fears that the new Government might start confiscating personal property roiled the property markets. The property markets crashed and the investment was lost. Now in his mid-60s without a retirement plan, Uncle Dennis climbed on board one of the heralded flights to Miami in an attempt to rebuild his life in the USA. His wife, Aunt Faye, was already succumbing to Alzheimer's, so he left her behind with their third son and took the only job that his circumstances allowed – work on an assembly line in Fort Lauderdale. With his business background, he soon saw ways to improve the efficiency of the operations and was quickly promoted to supervisor. By then Aunt Faye had died and he married his long-time companion, Blondie. Through the 1980s and 90s he earned enough to finally retire, but was beset by ailments. He suffered from multiple heart attacks and towards the end, Ronnie, his third son, decided to bring him back and care for him in Jamaica. Ronnie and my brother Chris had gone to medical school together and Chris had been treating Dennis in Florida for one of his many ailments. Chris called me to say that Dennis was headed back to Jamaica, that he was not doing well, and I should make sure to drop in and see him on my next trip there.

I arrived at Ronnie's house to find Dennis on a hospital bed that had been set up in the living room. Ronnie was on his way out the door on a fishing trip and asked that I keep an eye on him. Dennis did not immediately recognize me since it had been thirty years since we last saw each other. He quickly warmed up when he realized who I was. We had a very enjoyable conversation of over three hours, where, after updating each other on the last thirty years he told me how proud he was of his five boys and how happy he had been in his second marriage. His condition was obviously bad, though, and I could sense the fear that he felt. I bade him goodbye, fully realizing that this was likely the very last time I would see him alive. He died early the next week, and the following weekend I sadly found myself in that little church at Rock Hall.

It was a humble yet beautiful little chapel that sat proudly on the spine of the highest ground in the area. It was built of the finest cut white limestone, as were so many of the elegant old buildings in Jamaica. The roof showed the mismatch of painted and unpainted galvanized sheet roofing that probably came from hurried post-hurricane salvage of the flotsam of many owners' lost roofs. The view was panoramic with the north coast off to one side and Kingston Harbour off to the other. The driveway carved a full circle as it climbed up this conical, wind-swept hill, spiralling to the small parking lot at the back of the chapel. A field of wind-rippled Seymour grass attended by a herd of goats surrounded the chapel, reminding one of the poverty of the parish. With doors thrown wide open to the fresh breezes that are a constant in the island, there was no need for fans or air conditioning. The elderly parish priest whom we knew from the '60s in Spanish Town, Fr. Grenier, was one of the few surviving relics of the Boston-Irish priests that had dominated the pre-independent Jamaican Roman Catholic parishes.

The church was decked out in the trappings of the previous week's harvest service. Sugar cane and banana plants hung limply over the main door and surrounded the altar and I thought them fitting symbols of Dennis' earlier life as a sugar cane farmer. My eyes moved to the area in front of the altar where I expected to find a coffin. A small urn on a small table was all that was left of this man of ninety years, a man I spent a morning with a week before as his confidence had faded in the face of a death he knew was close. Was that all that could be expected at the end of a full life of four score years? A tiny urn and few friends and relatives?

The front pew held his second wife of some 25 years. She was a Jamaican Chinese woman, feared by many middle-class mid-century Caucasian Jamaican women. Beautiful Chinese and Indian girls were seen as home wreckers who used their beauty and charm to attract financially successful husbands. This was of course far from true and the parents of these girls did not at all approve of interracial relationships. After Aunt Faye died and Dennis had fallen on hard times, she had been his unwavering companion.

The oldest son was too busy in Belize to attend his dad's funeral. The second son and wife were forbidden by their new religion from entering the church of their old religion and sat in their cars in the parking lot. His many upper class white friends in Kingston could not take time from a Saturday's golf or horse racing to attend to someone that had fallen. Was it the fall from social class, or did the wives still hold raw the marital indiscretion of forty years hence? Apparently there was no forgiveness in these of a redemption-based faith. Yet there were faithful friends of another class, era, religion and race that would not have missed this for the world. Redemption was at hand. In a sad irony to the beautiful violin piece being played, this swan had become an ugly duckling in the eyes of his peers – but not to those humble souls in attendance.

Chapter twenty-four

Epilogue

B rowndale was sold in 1968 and my parents moved in retirement to a Kingston suburb, where they turned the large back yard into a giant rose garden. In 1974 they moved to Canada to be close to Geraldine and then in 1980 moved to Florida. Monica died in 1987 and Basil in 1988.

The other persons mentioned in this book have moved on and many migrated during the socialist years of the 1970's. My oldest sister, Geraldine, inherited her father's deep intellect and went off to university in Canada in 1960. She became a veterinarian and is now retired after a landmark career in research, first at Sick Children's Hospital in Toronto and then at the University of Western Ontario in London, Ontario.

My brother Christopher became a Physician, interned in Trinidad and after spending a few years in the Bahamas, settled down as a well loved, if somewhat eccentric, dermatologist in Boca Raton, Florida. He retired in 2004 after many years as a popular standout in that community, where, like our dad, has little interest in the trappings of wealth and is a lot happier mingling with people who are of humble means.

Paul (the author) left Jamaica in a 1976 job transfer to Trinidad and in 1979 moved with his family to Nassau Bahamas and later in another a job transfer, to Raleigh, North Carolina. He ran a software company for twenty years and then with his younger sister, Mary, co-founded a non-profit named Trees That Feed Foundation. This foundation is charged with the introduction of tree crops to tropical countries, starting with Jamaica. In 2009 they are introducing three Samoan varieties of breadfruit to Jamaica with the goal of extending the fruiting season to the complete year and bringing back breadfruit as a staple to the island. They have ambitious plans to extend operations, funded by donations, to other countries in the Caribbean Basin and West Africa. Paul has few of his parent's better qualities.

Rosalind migrated to Scotland in 1966 to become a nurse, worked at the Royal Infirmary then married the love of her life and lives in Edinburg. Plucked from home at an early age, she did not have a chance to fully embrace Jamaica and lives vicariously through Paul's stories. Rosy nonetheless has had a colourful life, spending summer holidays in Jamaica as a nurse in interesting posting like the Playboy Club Hotel. She passed on the adventurous spirit to her daughter, Katie, who is a wandering medic with Doctors without Borders. Katie has spent time in disaster-areas such as Kashmir after an earthquake; The Congo with war refugees; Sri Lanka with war refugees and in India at an orphanage. Rosy shares her mother's interest in humanity and a large part of her dad's sense of humour.

Mary married early, became a geologist and after job transfers to the Bahamas, moved with her family to Texas where she became a petroleum geologist. She now lives in Chicago and owns a business that makes hand-painted porcelain gift boxes and other commemoration gifts. Her boxes have been sold through Saks and are listed with the White House, the Mayor of Chicago's office and many other places. She is associated with the National Tropical Botanical Garden in Hawaii, from whence the breadfruit trees from Samoa will be sourced. She is a standout personality who has a strong sense of duty to give back to needy communities.

Our cousin Stephen grew up as one of the family. He became a lawyer, gained a reputation as one of the fairest in Jamaica, and moved in retirement to the wine country of northern California.

Cousin Robin moved to Grand Cayman in the '70s then migrated to the west coast of Florida, where he runs a garden service business. His brother Anthony has lived in Grand Cayman since the 1970's where he is now retired, lecturing part time at a local college.

Cousin Raymond Sowley became a lawyer, practiced in Trinidad and has now retired in Canada.

Ronnie DuQuesnay attended medical school with Christopher and became a top surgeon in Jamaica. His brother Desmond joined the British Army in 1963 and after serving in Europe returned to Jamaica in the late 1960s.

Uncle Cliff retired from the St. Anns Bay Parish Council and served the Jamaica Family Planning Institute for years. He is buried in the cemetery of his old church at Lauriston. Some years later on a family reunion trip to Jamaica dad asked Geraldine's husband, Gordon, to take him to see his dear brother's grave. Cliff and Basil had been close throughout their lives, and in fact looked so much alike that there was no missing the family resemblance. After a solemn few minutes at the tomb, dad hopped over the stone wall onto the Chalky Hill main road, where the car was parked. An old congregant happened to be walking past the church at the very same time and mistaking dad for Cliff, blurted out "A'parson duppy to backside!" and fled in the opposite direction. That impish man Cliff would have loved the humor in that little incident.

Virtue family in 1910. Dorothy, Teach, Basil, Helen, Sybil, Mistress, Alan and Cliff. Unknown lady at back right.

Great, Great Grandfather Noel Crosswell 1866

Kelly Family in 1926.

The younger generation of Virtues - Browndale - 1957
Paul, Geraldine, Christopher, Stephen (cousin), Rosalind, Mary

Chalky Hill, Jamaica – A view from near the Manse

Plumb Point Sunset – near Port Royal

Just after Before Day a' Mawnin' – a Jamaican sunrise at Boscobel

The Royal Poinciana's vibrant, orchid-like red flowers only emerge after a long dry period.

Port Antonio West Harbour and Navy Island. This was the first banana port and a late 19th century tourist destination. Navy Island was once owned by Errol Flynn, the movie actor.

Nearly all of Jamaica's 365 rivers rise from deep blue springs. The Roaring River, pictured here, is less than a mile long and falls a thousand feet in elevation from its source, a beautiful blue hole. Sadly, all but a hundred yards has been diverted for hydro-electric power generation.

Entrance to Boston Bay in Portland, named for the New England tourist trade with New England in the late 1800s and early 1900s

Dunn's River Falls is a less spectacular waterfall than Roaring River and has escaped its fate.

The Beach at Mamee Bay

Mamee Bay sunrise. The remnants of offshore thunderstorms ride the Trade Winds on summer nights, giving spectacular light shows.

Blue Mountain Peak looking towards Port Royal

Giant Silk Cotton (Kapok) tree at Dornoch River. These were used to make dugout canoes. This particular tree survived because it was miles from the sea.

A cattle ranch in St. Ann, showing ubiquitous stone wall

A new day in Ocho Rios

Iron sugar boiling pan – used to make cane sugar in earlier centuries

Giddy House at Port Royal tilted by 1907 earthquake

Before Day a' Mawnin' Page | 217

Paul in the Blue Mountains 1965

Maiden Cay – one of the beautiful islands off the south coast

Before Day a' Mawnin' Page | 218

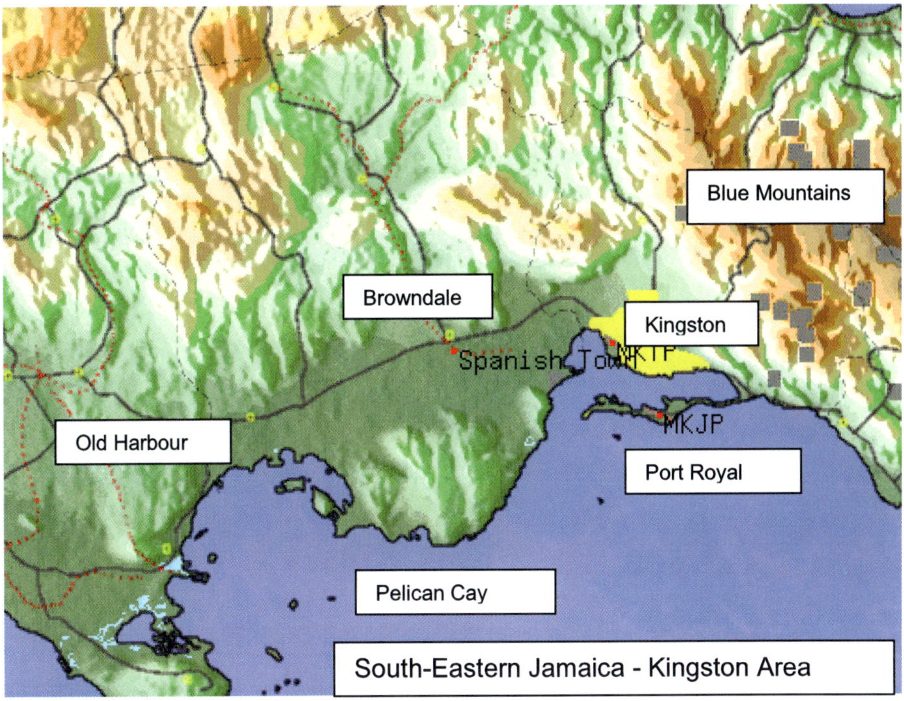

Blue Mountains
Browndale
Kingston
Spanish Town
MKTP
Old Harbour
MKJP
Port Royal
Pelican Cay
South-Eastern Jamaica - Kingston Area

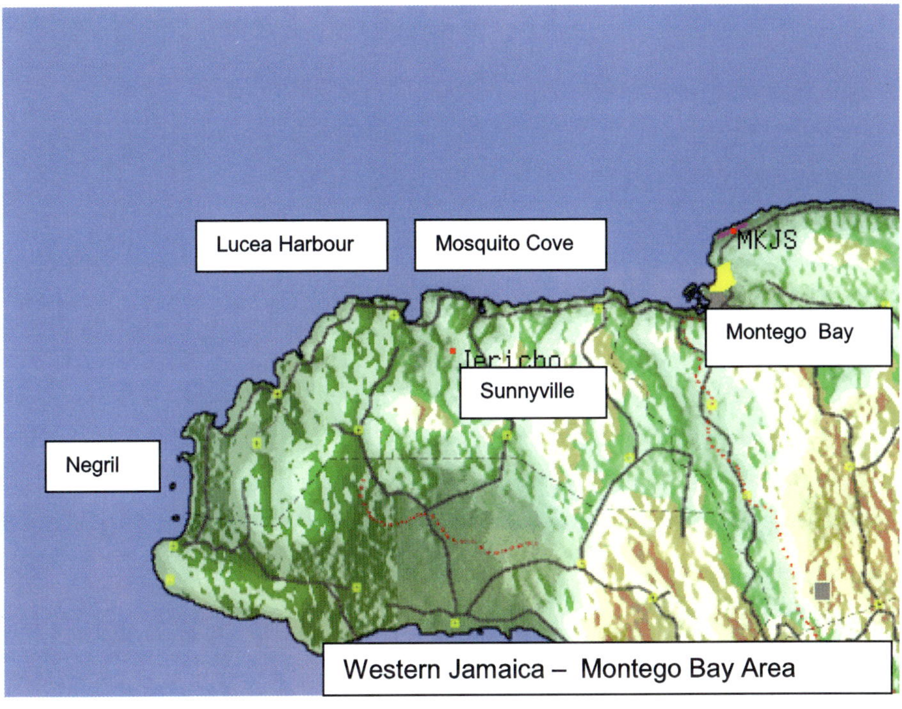

Lucea Harbour
Mosquito Cove
MKJS
Montego Bay
Jericho
Sunnyville
Negril
Western Jamaica – Montego Bay Area

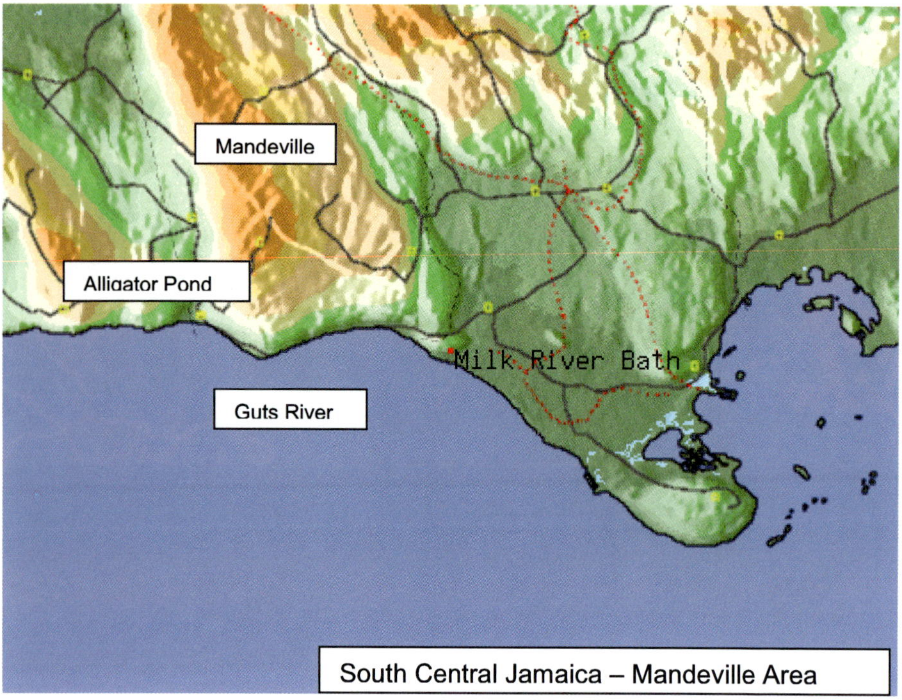

Mandeville

Alligator Pond

Guts River

Milk River Bath

South Central Jamaica – Mandeville Area

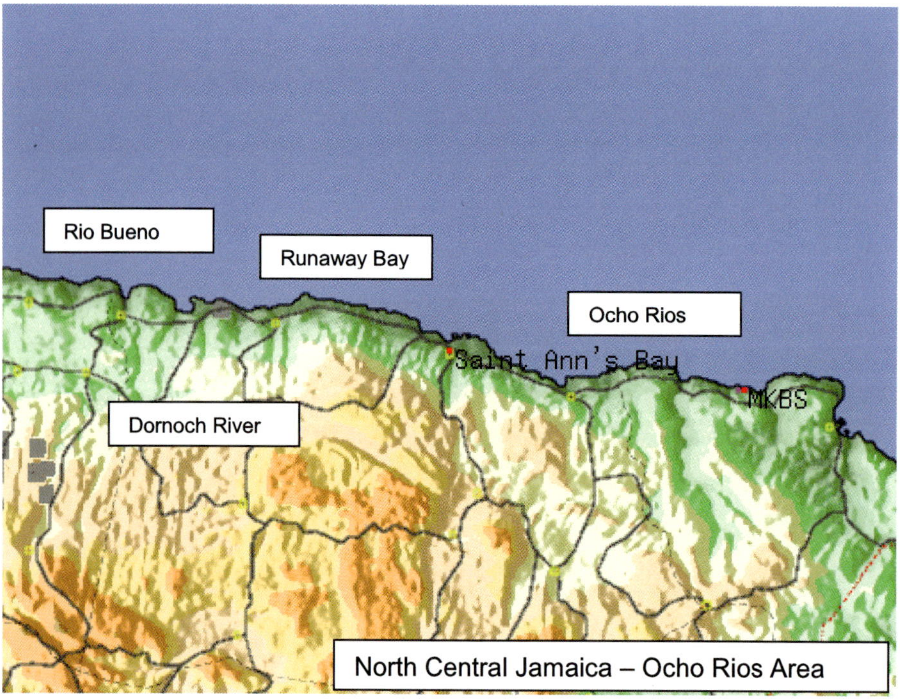

Rio Bueno

Runaway Bay

Ocho Rios

Saint Ann's Bay

MKBS

Dornoch River

North Central Jamaica – Ocho Rios Area

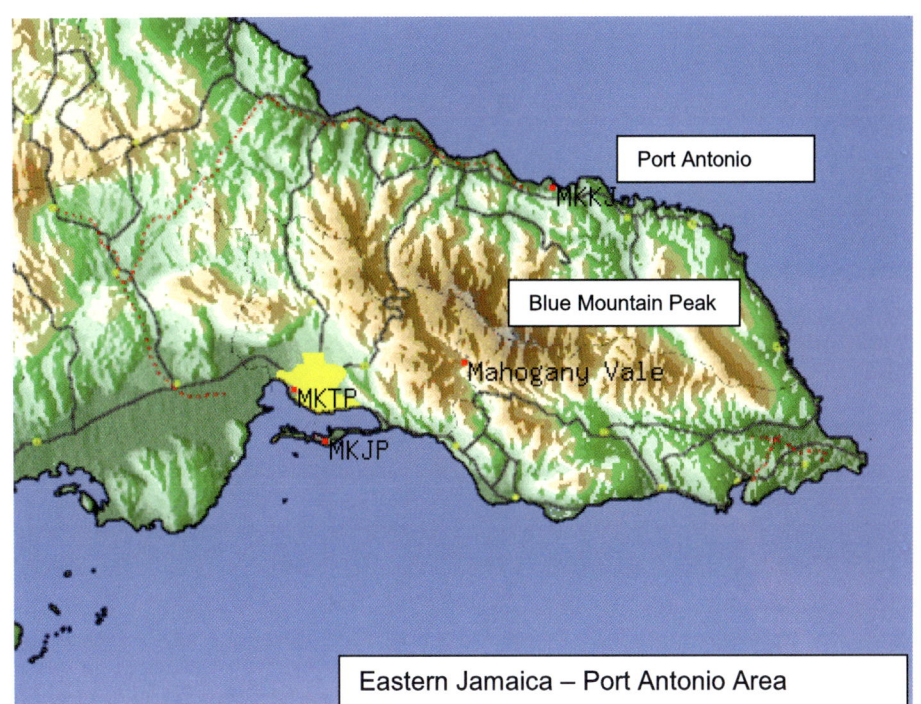

Eastern Jamaica – Port Antonio Area